The Contemplative Life

The Contemplative Life

Thomas Philippe, O.P.

Translated from the French by
Carmine Buonaiuto

Edited by Edward D. O'Connor, C.S.C.

CROSSROAD · NEW YORK

1990

The Crossroad Publishing Company
370 Lexington Avenue, New York, N.Y. 10017

Printed in the United States of America

Library of Congress Cataloging-in-Publication Data

Philippe, Thomas, 1905–
The contemplative life / Thomas Philippe ; translated from the
French and edited by Edward D. O'Connor.
   p.   cm.
"This work was originally conceived as a retreat and preached in
French to a Dominican community"—Editor's pref.
  ISBN 0-8245-0984-6
  1. Retreats. 2. Contemplation. I. O'Connor, Edward D. (Edward
Dennis) II. Title.
BX2375.P49 1990
248.8'94—dc20   89-22155
                                         CIP

Contents

Foreword by Henri J. M. Nouwen

The first time I met Père Thomas Philippe, O.P., was during the celebration of the Eucharist in the l'Arche community in the French village of Trosly-Breuil. It was in the fall of 1983. Père Thomas was the celebrant; I was the concelebrant.

I remember this first encounter very vividly. It was an encounter in prayer. He was very present to me, to the many handicapped persons and their assistants who surrounded him and, most of all, to God. He was a man on fire, the fire of God's Spirit. The way he pressed his eyes closed while praying silently, the intensity of the high pitched voice with which he said the prayers, read the Gospel, and proclaimed God's Word, the trembling hands stretched out over the bread and wine, the intimate way in which he gave communion to all who walked up to the altar . . . were all expressions of a man whose whole being had been transformed by the fire of God's love.

As I stood beside him behind the large rock that was the altar of the Trosly-Breuil chapel, I sensed that I was in the presence of a man in whom immense suffering and immense joy had become one. I knew that people from all over France, very simple and very sophisticated people, very poor and very wealthy people, young and old people, came to visit and listen to him. From early in the morning to late at night, there were

people sitting in the small waiting room in front of his her-
mitagelike living space. I knew that this old priest, in his
eighties, hard of hearing, slow in walking, unable to celebrate
without a tall chair to support him, and fragile in health, was
an immense source of faith, hope, and love for countless men
and women who experienced deep inner darkness. I knew
Père Philippe was as much a starets as any Western monk has
ever been. What Father Zosina had been for Dostoevski in
nineteenth-century Rome, Père Thomas was for many in
twentieth-century France.

During 1983 and 1984, I had often celebrated the Eucharist
with Père Thomas, but never felt a desire to spend much
personal time with him. When I saw the many visitors waiting
to see him, I realized that he would be there for me when I
truly needed him. In fact, I was somewhat hesitant to go to
him. His sermons, his prayerful presence during the common
worship, and his friendly greetings had given me enough
spiritual nourishment, and I felt that I would be wasting his
time by asking him questions in sharing my problems.

But all of this changed when two years later, in the fall of
1986, I began to experience a deeper anguish than I had ever
experienced before. The anguish had appeared in the context
of my life with the mentally handicapped in the l'Arche community in Toronto. It was during that time that I was invited
to come back to Trosly to make a retreat guided by Père
Thomas, together with the other priests of l'Arche. I went and
poured out my anguished heart to the old priest. And right
then and there he became for me the most tangible manifesta-
tion of God's compassion I had ever experienced. It seemed
that the depth of my inner pain had called forth from him the
depth of God's compassion. He had important things to say,
some of the things I had heard before in his sermons; he had
good advice to offer, some of it I had heard from others too; he
was generous with his time, a generosity that I had experienced before. What was new was not his generosity, his advice

and insight, but his luminous presence. It seemed that healing came not from what he said, but directly from his own
heart. It seemed that the fire of God's Spirit, the healing
warmth of God's love, the softening touch of God's hands,
were there for me. As I let my agony and anguish become
visible to him, he became my father, my mother, my brother,
my sister, my lover, my God. While being with him, I knew
what true consolation was. I sensed that none of my pain was
alien to him, and none of my tears unfamiliar to him.

Père Thomas usually speaks much and explains much, but
in the presence of my struggle he was silent, though with a
silence so full of love that I did not want to leave him. He
made me sit very close to him and, after a period of few words,
he invited me to pray with him. He put his head against my
shoulder and entered into a deep silence. An outsider might
think he had fallen asleep, but I knew and felt that he was
bringing the healing Spirit of God right into the brokenness of
my heart. After fifteen minutes of silence, he looked up at me
and asked, "Are you feeling any better?" I said "Yes," not
because my anguish was gone, but because somehow Père
Thomas had through himself connected my anguish with the
anguish of Jesus, and made me aware that I would be able to
live through it. When I left him, he said, "If you wake up in
the middle of the night and your anguish overwhelms you,
think of me." He did not say, "Think of God" or "Think of
Jesus." He said "Think of me." He said it with such gentleness
and compassion, so free from any self-preoccupation or self-
importance, that I realized that he offered himself as the safe
way to the healing presence of Jesus. Père Thomas Philippe
knew more, much more, about suffering than I did, and he
had lived it through in faith. That was the source of his
authority; it was also the source of his compassion.

After this profound experience, I realized that it is rather
unimportant to know much about Père Thomas's personal
past. I had heard that he had been a professor of theology in

Paris, that he had started an ecumenical community, Eau Vive, that he had suffered many forms of misunderstanding and rejection, that he had lived for many years in Trosly-Breuil and had started there to care for the elderly and the mentally handicapped. I had also heard that he was the spiritual father of Jean Vanier and had been his main inspiration in starting l'Arche. But these are only a few of the many events that shaped his life. Now it seems that personal history is more a barrier than the way to a deeper understanding of this holy priest. Meeting him is meeting a man so full of the Spirit of God that facts and figures are only distractions. He has become a living flame of God's love. There is no need to be important, no desire to be acclaimed, no clinging to a "curriculum vitae," no holding on to trophies of the past. They all seem to be only shadows that prevent the light of God's love from shining brightly. In his old age, he became what he most wanted to be, a man transparent to the presence of God.

Although Père Thomas Philippe has influenced many people in a very radical way, Jean Vanier among them, he has remained quite unknown outside France. His books, most of them transcriptions of his taped retreats and sermons, seldom found their way beyond the borders of his own country. It is, therefore, a unique event that Father O'Connor has made this theological retreat about the contemplative life available in the English language. Father O'Connor knows Père Thomas in ways few others do. For many years he has come to Trosly and listened to Père Thomas and let his heart be touched by him. This translation is thus the work of a true disciple, a man who knows and loves his master and wants no more than that his master will touch the hearts of many as deeply as he touched his own.

Jean Vanier met Père Thomas in 1947, Father Ed O'Connor came to know him in 1948, and only in 1983 did I encounter him. Our lives, different as they are, have been deeply influenced by this holy priest. I even dare to say that Jean, Ed, and myself cannot speak about our spiritual journey without acknowledging the crucial role Père Thomas played in it. I hope and pray that this text will give the reader a glimpse of the man we know and love.

Foreword by Jean Vanier

I met Father Thomas Philippe for the first time in 1947. He was a friend of my father, who was then the Canadian ambassador to France. However, I only really got to know him in 1950, when I resigned from the Royal Canadian Navy. Not knowing quite what Jesus wanted of me, I felt it would be good to spend a year in a place of prayer and study, a place where I could prepare myself to follow Jesus more closely.

And so it was that I went to Eau Vive, a community near Paris, founded by Father Thomas soon after the end of the war. There people from many countries came to learn to pray, to study philosophy and theology, and to live a community life—and all this in a spirit of poverty. The community did not have much money, so each person had to work hard to keep the place going. The rather austere life of Eau Vive was not difficult for me; life in the navy had been quite hard. But there was something new here: it was a place of meeting with Jesus.

I would assist each day at the Mass of Father Thomas. I followed his classes in theology at the nearby Dominican house of studies. I would listen to the spiritual talks he gave to us in the community. I also would often chauffeur him when he gave talks and sometimes retreats in various contemplative convents or monasteries. It was while listening to him that I received my first graces of prayer. It was as if Jesus was transforming my heart and leading me into a new and deeper love of the Father. This new inner life linked me obviously very deeply to Father Thomas but it also gradually gave me a great inner freedom; it helped me become myself in a new and deeper way.

In 1952, Father Thomas left Eau Vive. It was some eleven years later that I again met him in a little village northeast of Paris. My journey had continued. I had acquired a doctorate in philosophy. His journey had also continued; he was then living close to persons who had suffered. He was the priest for a small institution for men with mental handicaps. As previously he had introduced me into a life of prayer through revealing to me the hearts of Jesus and Mary, here he introduced me to this world of suffering, and to these men who had been rejected because of their handicap. Shortly after, invited and encouraged by Father Thomas, I settled in this village, close to this institution, and close to Father Thomas. I bought a small, dilapidated house and welcomed into it two men with mental handicaps who had been living in a rather dismal asylum south of Paris. We started living together. Thus l'Arche was born. And over the years the communities of l'Arche have grown throughout the world. And with them has grown in me and in others a consciousness of the spirituality that is at the heart of l'Arche: a union with Jesus hidden in the poor. Father Thomas has continued to accompany me and many others in l'Arche and especially many persons with handicaps. He has helped me to grow in the love of Jesus through the love of Mary and always to remain centered upon the essential.

Father Thomas had given this present retreat before I met him. I read it shortly after my arrival in Eau Vive. It helped me a lot. The theological aspect of this retreat gave me the intellectual understanding in faith of what was happening inside me and in my heart. It helped me to trust more in the

Holy Spirit within my own heart and to let myself "be seized" by Christ.

Some readers will be surprised at what Father Thomas calls "preaching from the heart."[1] Many might have had an experience of preaching that touched their hearts and brought about in them a real conversion. A small number may have had an experience of listening to spiritual talks, which led them into an experience of the love of Jesus in silence, into mystical prayer. This was my experience, an experience that changed my life and brought me to the understanding I have today of the Good News of Jesus. It is this mystical prayer that is the center of the contemplative life that has flourished in the Catholic Church over the centuries and finds its expression not only in the many monasteries, hermitages, and contemplate convents all over the world, but in the hearts of people hidden in all the villages and cities of our lands, hidden in the hearts too of the elderly and of those who are sick and handicapped. There are many hidden contemplatives in our world.

The theology of Father Thomas has evolved since 1950. Today his words are perhaps simpler, more concrete; for over twenty years now he has been living in a community where there are so many with a mental handicap. His words at every Mass are for us all, but without any doubt they touch deeply the hearts of the poorest among us. And of course he himself has learned much from them, from Jesus living in them. But the essential has not changed. This theological retreat is important for it brings us to the heart of the mystery of the Word made flesh. The message of Jesus is a message of love. Jesus came to reveal to us the Father. He came to lead us into an experience of love, of the Trinity, in faith. Christianity is not first of all a social message or a struggle for justice; it is not first of all "doing good to the poor"; it is an experience of God, an experience of love that is a free gift and brings us to inner freedom. This gift transforms us, liberates us from fear, and from guilt and sin; it makes us children of the Father and friends, brothers and sisters of Jesus. Prayer is receiving in one's heart the heart of Jesus: Jesus teaching us how he loves the Father and how he loves every person, particularly the littlest and the weakest. "As the Father loves me, so I love you, and my commandment is that you love one another as I love you."

I trust and hope that this retreat of Father Thomas will help many as it helped me; and that it will lead many into the paths of prayer where we can remain and rest in his love, and thus bear much fruit, for the glory of the Father.

Editor's Preface

The contemplative life received little attention in this country before Thomas Merton. Through his work, it came very much into vogue; but this has often led to its being confused with other things. Poetic contemplation, worthy though it be in its own domain, ought not to be taken for that divine contemplation, *contemplatio infusa,* from which the contemplative life is named. Moments of stillness and reflection are indispensable for the maintenance of a "life worth living," but are not to be equated with the prayer of quiet. Profound intuitions, exquisite sensitivity, and tender compassion are among the most precious human realities, but when a compulsively psychologizing culture identifies them with contemplation, it is a gross counterfeit.

The present work is one of the purest and most authentic statements I know of the classic doctrine on the contemplative life. It comes out of a rich and ancient tradition that takes its chief insights from great mystics such as Teresa and John, Catherine of Siena, Francis de Sales, and others all the way back to Cassian and Dionysius, and right on down to some of the still-hidden mystics of our own day. Its articulation comes largely from the Thomistic school, not only as represented by Garrigou-Lagrange (under whom Father Philippe studied and with whom he taught for a while at the Angelicum), but also from Pierre-Thomas Dehau, O.P.,[1] and through him from a long, well-tested French Dominican tradition that has forged a fine, sensitive idiom for the elusive realities of the interior life.

This tradition, which has hardly penetrated the English-speaking world, has almost disappeared today even in France. Nevertheless, for those who have ears to hear, it is still luminous and liberating. And Father Philippe, who knows by personal experience whereof he speaks, adds a touch of concrete realism and unexpected originality to what could otherwise become trite maxims.

Reading this work will not be without difficulty. The author at times takes for granted axioms that surprise us, and assumes, without explanation, positions we may be reluctant to grant. A few truly old-fashioned notions compound the difficulty, but hardly affect the substance of the doctrine.

Not all that Father Philippe says is suitable for everyone. He writes for contemplatives; if some of his views are not applicable to persons of an active psychology (thus especially chapter 13), this is to be expected. He writes also in the perspective of graces that have not been given even to all contemplatives; however, they deserve to be respected even when they are not shared.

This work was originally conceived as a retreat and preached in French to a Dominican community. Careful notes taken by a retreatant served as the basis of the present translation, which was made originally by Carmine Buonaiuto and revised by myself. I was impressed by the completeness and precision of the notes. Nevertheless, being only notes on an unwritten discourse, they often consist of laconic phrases rather than complete sentences (particularly at the end of each conference, where the speaker was winding up with an exhortation). They needed therefore to be edited before being published, and Father Philippe generously authorized me to do this.

The editorial work has been very modest. I have suppressed a few sentences or phrases, either because their meaning was not fully clear, or occasionally because, for one reason or another, they no longer seemed appropriate. Those of any significance have been indicated in notes. In order to prevent the universality of the message from being obscured, specific references to the Dominicans have been replaced by more general references to "contemplatives" whenever what was said was of general application. (But when something proper to the Dominicans was at issue, the specific reference was retained.) Occasionally, the order of sentences or paragraphs has been altered. This too is pointed out in the notes. A few changes in language were made, but only when they seemed clearly in accord with the author's intent. All the notes are my work, except for note 1 of chapter 9, as is there explained.

My overriding concern has been to present faithfully the thought of a holy man whom I venerate as perhaps the finest interpreter of Christian spirituality in modern times. Nowhere have I interjected any independent ideas of my own. Nevertheless, because of the delicate nature of editing the work of someone unable to review what has been done, I take responsibility for the text as it now stands.

One other work by Father Philippe has already appeared in English (*The Fire of Contemplation,* translated by Sister Verda Clare Doran, CSC, Alba House, 1981). The introduction to it gives some biographical background, which need not be repeated here. A third book, tentatively entitled *Mary, Model of the Contemplative Life,* is expected to appear very soon. Of the three, the present work is the most basic and systematic, and would serve as the best introduction to the others.

I am particularly grateful for the self-effacing helpfulness of Carmine Buonaiuto who did the hardest part of the translation, and then allowed me to rework it in the way that seemed best. He is an exemplar of many of the qualities proposed in this book.

Likewise I owe abundant thanks to Mrs. Cheryl Reed, Mrs.

Nancy Kegler, Mrs. Nila Gerhold, and Mrs. Shirley Vogel of the Faculty Steno Pool at Notre Dame, who typed the manuscript. Their patience with the many revisions through which it passed was edifying.

Edward D. O'Connor, C.S.C.

1

Retreat: A Mystery of Purification, Illumination, and Union

A retreat is said to be a "spiritual exercise." This is especially true of a retreat for contemplatives, for whom it should be a moment of particularly intense spiritual life. The spirit that ought to animate this exercise is the Spirit of Jesus, the Holy Spirit. If a retreat is to be fruitful, it must be essentially the work of the Holy Spirit. Hence we should approach the retreat with very great humility as something that is beyond us; it will be vain if the Holy Spirit does not intervene.

The intervention of the Holy Spirit is likewise necessary in order for the word of the preacher to be really the word of God. What we are about to experience together is a mystery. All preaching is a mystery, somewhat analogous to the sacraments. Our Lord willed to communicate his life through these two means of the sacraments and preaching; thus, when commissioning the apostles, he told them, "Go, teach all nations, and baptize them. . . ."

For a convent of contemplatives, the retreat is the greatest

1

moment of the year as far as preaching is concerned—Our Lord's great sermon to the community, a time of very intense common life in which the preacher lives the mystery of preaching together with his listeners. It is a moment when we will be living a unique aspect of the mystery of the communion of saints.

Of itself the contemplative life calls for solitude. If it also requires community life, this is because of the need to practice virtue. But in itself the contemplative life is something hidden; its secret life is realized in the innermost depths of our souls.

The particular value of a retreat lies in the fact that in it the contemplative life becomes a common life. The preacher, borne by his hearers, expresses and exteriorizes what is hidden in the depths of their souls. Thus occurs a mysterious communal sharing of personal treasures, as all bring to the retreat their own special graces. They should come likewise with their deepest needs, so that the preacher might be drawn out, as it were, by them. Apostles will be led by the Holy Spirit to give to those whose thirst is greater much more than they themselves had prepared; and to others much more than they were ready to ask for, thus causing them to profit too.

We should come to the retreat, then, with great simplicity and magnanimity as well as faith in this mystery. We are awaiting the word of the Lord.

Like the sacraments, preaching is situated on the plane of the theological virtues. That is why it is a mystery. The profit we derive from it will consequently be proportionate to the depth of our faith, hope, and love.

Let us entrust this mystery to the Blessed Virgin Mary, that she may envelop us with her prayer and enlighten us. This was her role among the Apostles in the Cenacle where the mystery of preaching began.

The mystery of preaching is at one and the same time a

mystery of purification, illumination, and unity. In real life, the Holy Spirit does not separate these three functions; but we have to make distinctions in order better to analyze the mystery.

Purification

Purification means first of all gaining a more intense awareness of our vocation. It is not a matter of recalling the thoughts we may have had at the time we took the habit or made our profession. At the beginning of our religious life, we had an imprecise and very human conception of our vocation. But as we live the contemplative life, we acquire a deeper and deeper understanding of it (albeit more obscure, for it is a mystery).

Hence every year we need to renew our personal awareness of our vocation. Not by a perfunctory reminder, but by suspending our secondary activities in order to allow the more essential ones—those bound up with the very essence of the contemplative life—to expand fully. In other words, we ought to become more fully aware of the end that God wills for us and of the means by which God wills us to attain this end. That is to say, we should realize the special love that God and Jesus have for us.

In light of this end we will be able to discern those human things from which we must become detached in order to fulfill this vocation and attain this end. We must be very faithful in respect to these detachments. Sometimes God gives us a mere presentiment of them, and we have only prudential judgments to go by, not certitude. We must go forward then in faith. We should ask for counsel but then courageously undertake the detachments that appear necessary. Later on we will see better.

Let us note in passing that those who are devoted to the spiritual life experience the same states of soul and the same trials as those who are in the process of conversion, only on a different level. For the latter the last moments before conversion are often the darkest. Only after the step is taken does the light come, and they feel "at home." The contemplative experiences the very same thing on the spiritual plane. There is a mysterious affinity between the contemplative and the sinner. Hence an apostle needs to have an intense contemplative life in order to understand the psychology of sinners and searchers so that he can help them.

Let us, therefore, ask God to show us the obstacles that hinder us from discerning our true vocation. May he detach us and purify us so that we may be able to see and realize—in other words, to love. The retreat is the great examination of conscience of the year, but we should make it in a contemplative manner. A very contemplative way to make it is to go before Our Lord in an attitude of humility and ask him to purify us himself. Then he will be the one who makes this examination in us.

But it should be the examination of conscience of a free child, before the face of God. It is a very good thing to feel the demands that God makes upon us. Pride is what stands in the way of God's giving himself to us, and God has to enlighten us to see this obstacle. Likewise, it must be God and the Blessed Virgin who "reproach" us. Nothing could be more crucifying, yet nothing is sweeter. May they lay bare our involuntary faults. For, as St. Thomas teaches, there are involuntary sins, and they wound the heart of Our Lord. (We can see this better if we recall that in friendship the hurt is not lessened when the one who hurt us says, "I wasn't paying attention!" This is precisely what wounds! One who does not pay attention is hardly a friend!)

We should never seek to justify ourselves; for the Holy Spirit is a very sensitive friend. We should ask the Spirit for light and be very grateful when we begin to receive it.

Illumination

Illumination is already beginning to occur in purification, but it has a further aspect. In making us more deeply aware of our goal, the Holy Spirit also gives us a very pure and elevated vision of the grandeur of our vocation and ideal. To see clearly, one must look at the mountaintops.

From the practical point of view of living out our ideal, this work of illumination is all the more important because the ideal we strive for is what gives our life its value. We will be judged by our intentions. But there is a great temptation to lower our ideal so that it will not stand in judgment over us. *That* is the sin against the light. To sin against the Holy Spirit is to lower one's ideal, to renounce it, to allege that we are not made for that, that there are other things to do, and so forth. Thus, we close ourselves off, and the Holy Spirit can no longer intervene in our lives. This does not usually come about by a single harsh action, but little by little, without our noticing it. This is what we must reexamine during a retreat.

The Work of Union

Our Lord is present. We are not here merely to absorb something for later on; we must live our contemplative life to the full during the retreat. The retreat is above all a work of charity. We must listen to Jesus in a spirit of prayer, as Mary did at Bethany.

Our chief effort should be to try to realize this mystery of charity and unity with God and with one another. Let us together form a collective contemplative entity. It is a special grace of God that makes, not just some individual souls, but the community itself rise to the level of contemplative life, be contemplative, and raise its members to the contemplative life. This is the grace we must ask for.

2

The Purpose of the Dominican Order

A renewed personal awareness of our vocation requires that we have a clear understanding of the purpose of our order. The Dominicans are by their very essence apostolic; that is, the apostolate is the sole reason for the existence of the friars, the cloistered nuns, and the Third Order. In order better to discern the kind of interior life we ought to have, let us define this apostolic purpose more exactly.

In the Church there are contemplative, active, and apostolic orders—the last being both contemplative and active, or "mixed."

Apostolate is a word that can have several very different meanings. But we, like St. Thomas, should understand it in a very precise sense—namely, as "saving souls through preaching." We must also define exactly the characteristic note of this preaching. According to St. Thomas, there are several different kinds of preaching. *Apologetic* preaching dispels objections to the faith; *catechetical* preaching prepares people for the faith; *moral* preaching teaches them how to live their Christian life. The last two are typically the work of pastors and shepherds. Finally, there is *holy* preaching, which belongs properly to bishops but is delegated by them to the Preaching Friars. This last kind is supposed to give the secrets of the faith: it should be a doctrinal preaching, which above all

6

presents the dogmas and mysteries of the faith insofar as they are a *life*, a nourishment of the interior life. (Catechesis presents the dogmas merely as rudiments of the faith.)

Here we should note in passing the difference between active and contemplative personalities. The matter, so to speak, of the active life is the activity to which one is devoted. The father of a family or a doctor, for example, have the psychology proper to their activities. The contemplative, on the other hand, lives on the dogmas and the mysteries of the faith. They constitute the *matter* of his or her life and give him or her a kind of "divine" psychology.

The function of holy preaching, then, is to make us penetrate into the mysteries of the faith. It aims also to give us "the spirit of the Gospel" and make us live the Beatitudes. This means a life that corresponds, on the moral plane, to the mysteries of the faith.

That is the kind of preaching that was done by the Apostles. It is something truly mysterious—the kind of preaching that corresponds to the sacraments ("Go, teach . . . and baptize . . ." Jesus said to the Apostles). It was peculiar to the twelve Apostles and is not to be found outside Catholicism. It needs, of course, to be complemented by apologetic, catechetical, and moral preaching.[1]

It is this holy preaching that our Lord entrusted to the sons of St. Dominic. According to St. Thomas, it is the proper function of bishops who, being in the state of perfection,[2] ought to be contemplatives.

This leads us to consider two conceptions of the apostolate, active and contemplative (the latter being the apostolate that arises out of contemplation).

THE ACTIVE APOSTOLATE

The active apostolate goes first to human beings; it goes to God through others. Just as we can reach God only through contemplation, we can reach other persons only through action. Human beings as such cannot be objects of contemplation (they can be so only in God). And there are two ways of working actively: by deeds (human realities) and by oratory. The latter refers to "active" preaching, in which the primary or specific concern is the preaching itself; that is how best to reach one's hearers and maintain contact with them.

The latter is perhaps more spiritual than such activities as the care of the sick, for it is completely directed toward God. It remains action nonetheless: the preacher goes out to souls in order to lead them back to God.

This is the attitude of a pastor inasmuch as he is entrusted with souls. He does not have the right to abandon any part of his flock. He is obliged to use every means to reach all the souls entrusted to him. It may therefore be necessary for him to have recourse to means that are very exterior and human (movies, dances, and the like); and he should use them.

But a preacher, an apostle who comes in only for a moment and is not charged with the ongoing care of souls, can carry on a purely contemplative type of preaching. (Similarly, a bishop, in order to reach all his flock, needs to be surrounded by aides and vicars who make use of active means.)

THE CONTEMPLATIVE APOSTOLATE

The contemplative apostolate is that which arises out of contemplation. Obviously no one can be a perfect apostle without some elements of contemplation. But there is a certain ministry that no one can fulfill unless the minister *is* a contemplative. Holy preaching by its very essence, per se, demands contemplation.

The sacraments are more divine than preaching. Nevertheless, *all* priests are ministers of the sacraments, whereas bishops alone are the proper ministers of holy preaching.[3] There is a mystery in this; by determining the gestures and words of the sacraments,[4] God made it unnecessary for their minister to be a contemplative. Grace is communicated regardless. But in preaching God makes use of the intelligence, heart, and mouth of the minister. God puts trust in the minister. That is why the latter needs to be a contemplative.

Arising out of contemplation, holy preaching should normally draw the listener toward contemplation. Consequently, the contemplative preacher turns first of all to God, and it is God who sends the preacher to souls. The preacher goes to God as a friend and a "useless servant."

As a friend: for God alone is and should be enough for him. If this were not so, he would not be God's friend. To be a contemplative preacher, one must be capable of living as a pure contemplative, one for whom God alone suffices. One engaged in the active life has a human psychology, but the contemplative preacher has a divine psychology. God is the life of his soul; people add only a nuance.

As a "useless servant" (Lk. 17:10): because he cannot be a true apostle of God—a contemplative apostle—unless he is a mere instrument. He must not desire to be helpful to God, he must be deeply aware that God does not need him and uses him only out of sheer kindness. Because the goods he ministers are divine, he cannot give them of himself but only as an instrument.

One whose vocation is to give human goods can have the psychology of a human servant, a "useful" servant. Not so, however, the one who brings divine goods. This calls for profound humility. In a word, the truly contemplative apostle will in a sense regret every least thought that is not about God.

To be sure, God can use apostolic motives to draw a person closer to himself; but this is only a first stage. We should accept such stimuli with humility and ask Our Lord to purify us so that more and more God alone may suffice for us, that God may be the object of our contemplation.

We often hear of the "consolations of the apostolate," but can we ever find rest anywhere but in Our Lord? This is especially the case for a priest called to be a contemplative. Those consolations ought to be accepted humbly, because we should take advantage of everything that can lead us to God; but they cast a little shadow on our life. The moment such human motives make themselves felt, we should ask Our Lord to purify us. We must have the loftiest conception of our ideal, but we do not have to lift ourselves up to it on our own; it is God who places us at the height he wishes. But we do have to beg God to purify us and make us more contemplative.

The Blessed Virgin is the one who can form the contemplative preacher in this style. Mary is the only saint who had a truly priestly heart (although not the priestly office); she was the mother of souls simply by being the bride of Our Lord's heart. She was completely concerned with him, completely given to him. At the Cross she received all humankind in the heart of Our Lord. This is why she is the model and ideal for the contemplative preacher.

If a preacher is a true contemplative, apostolic activity will be a cross. The only beatitude that St. Thomas attributes to the preacher is "Blessed are they who suffer persecution. . . ." And the normal end of persecution is martyrdom.

The psychology of an instrument necessarily involves a sort of death. In mind and heart, the preacher must be a crucified person, for action becomes contemplation only on the cross. Nothing but sacrifice (*sacrum facere*—"sacred action") is on the same level as contemplation. This shows how, in a contemplative perspective, the apostolate links up with the sacrifice of the Mass.

The apostolate adds sacrifice to contemplation; hence crosses are normal in an apostolate. They are the sign that God is sanctifying it and making it fruitful.

In our religious life likewise there is an aspect of sacrifice: the vows. They transform the activity inevitable in every human life into sacred action, sacrifice, and thus place it on the level of contemplation.

Since the contemplative apostle should act in the manner of an instrument, let us try to define the psychology of an instrument of God a little more precisely by contrasting it with the psychology of a "secondary cause."[5]

The secondary cause acts by virtue of its own nature; the instrument acts by virtue of the principal cause. The consequence is obvious: the instrument should be solicitous above all to remain in contact with the First Cause as closely as possible. Concern about making contact with the audience is secondary for him; it is the Principal Cause who will bring about that contact. What is above all necessary for the instrument is to remain in the presence of God, asking what *God* wants said and done. Hence, the preacher will say not what pleases the listener, but what God wants him to say. The secondary cause, on the other hand, will be chiefly concerned about audience contact.

This has many applications. The spirituality of an apostle ought to be the spirituality of a pure contemplative. Preaching is nothing other than a contemplative life overflowing and propagating itself; it requires therefore an intense contemplative life.

Moreover, the apostle is by his calling only an instrument; he has no personality of his own. It is God who leads him; all the more reason why he should remain closely united with God. The very demands of his ministry, then, require that he be doubly contemplative—if we may so put it. Contemplation is the duty of his state.

This means also that one can hope to attain a more deeply contemplative life in a mixed order than in a purely contemplative one, because God will give himself to the preacher not only as to a chosen soul but also for the sake of others.

To this contemplative spirituality must be joined a very great humility and spirit of sacrifice. A preacher who is afraid of the Cross and who wishes to avoid it cannot be an apostle. An apostle loves the Cross—the Cross of Our Lord—as St. Dominic did, not his own crosses (this would still be a little too human).

It might be objected that there are in the Church now new forms of evangelization, which make holy preaching no longer necessary. For example, the apostolate of "like by like," as used to be said of Catholic Action.[6] On the contrary, the different functions that become necessary as the Church develops do not supplant one another. The new kinds of evangelization only make it all the more necessary for Dominicans to specialize in holy preaching, because no other order has the responsibility to carry it on.

A conclusion that follows from the above is that apostles do not go looking for souls, but are sent to them by God. The apostle is something like an unmoved mover: he does not have to busy himself or be preoccupied about his apostolate or his influence. God uses instruments when God sees fit. God can allow a preacher's life to remain apparently sterile for years. For a contemplative the apostolate is not something quantitative. Preoccupation about having an effect on people is a sentiment characteristic of the active life.

Contemplation alone constitutes the interior life of the apostle. Contemplation, not apostolic concern, is the note that defines his psychology. The friar preacher is not a pastor; he does not have to supply all the needs of all the people of his time; there are other orders for that. In an attitude of humility, he must respond to the needs of those who are looking for contemplative preachers. (It is striking to observe today that, in order to touch the hearts of pagans and atheists, who have spiritualized their paganism, it is necessary to be a contemplative.[7])

3

The Mystery of the Contemplative Life

For Dominicans the apostolate is supposed to spring from the superabundance of contemplation. Our life, therefore, is essentially contemplative and it is the contemplative life particularly that we must examine. I will consider first the nature of the Christian contemplative life (chap. 3); second the special call to the contemplative life and the basic attitudes that it calls for (chap. 4), and third the Blessed Virgin, model of Christian contemplation (chap. 5).

THE CHRISTIAN CONTEMPLATIVE LIFE

Although I will conclude with some considerations about the Blessed Virgin, I must also begin with her, because in order to understand the contemplative life, it helps to see it in a concrete realization.

When considered theoretically, the contemplative life is a mystery. How is it possible to have contemplation in the darkness of faith?

But considered concretely, the contemplative life is Mary's life. She is the model of the contemplative life lived in faith.

Our Lord was, indeed, the chief contemplative; according to Catholic tradition, he enjoyed the beatific vision even while on earth. Mary, however, lived by faith just as we do, and she was the only pure creature ever to lead a completely perfect contemplative life. It follows naturally that contemplative life for us means to live as she did. All our questions can be answered by seeing how she lived. In our problems, it is enough to turn to her, for the role of the Church is to perpetute the life of the Blessed Virgin. Where the apostle has Christ for a model, the contemplative has Mary. For Mary was predestined to be the glorious Mother of God not only at the moment of the Incarnation, but for all eternity. (This shows the importance of the dogma of the Assumption.)

What, then, is the contemplative life? According to St. Augustine the active life belongs to time, the contemplative to eternity. It is also enlightening to reflect that the contemplative life is the *normal* life of grace. In the supernatural order, God has given us new capacities of life—the theological virtues as a participation in his own life, enabling us to live as God's children and friends, and to know the secrets of his life.

Man is capable of discovering by reason that God is not only his origin but also his last end (this is philosophy), and that everything within him ought to be ordered and directed to God (this is natural religion).

But God has raised us to the supernatural order and allowed us to come to know him in himself and not merely through his creatures. He has revealed to us the mystery of his inner life, the relationships of the divine Persons; and he has let us know at the same time that we are called to participate in that life as his children and friends.

These two revelations go together, for when someone is so intimate with us as to reveal the secrets of his life, it goes without saying that he wants to make us his friends; there is no need to say more. The very fact that God freely reveals to us the mystery of the trinitarian life, a secret that no created intellect could possibly discover, is enough to tell us that God wants to make us his children and friends. This is the treasure contained in the New Testament: God reveals to us the mystery of God's interior life, the mystery of the Holy Trinity, and lets us call him Father.

The contemplative life is the life that corresponds properly and specifically to the theological virtues; the life that seeks to stay on their level. It is the life in which one strives to live as a child and friend of God; it is a "theological," a divine life. (We take the word *life* in the sense of a specific occupation to which a person devotes himself. It is the object of all his concern, that to which he always returns and to which he relates everything else. Thus a mother is said to live *for* her children.)

For contemplatives, God is not merely the first principle and last end, but the direct object of our concern. We go to God directly and not through intermediaries, such as nature or the poor or other people. This is made possible by the theological virtues, which have God as their immediate object and thus have an eternal value. The principal, specific and, so to speak, professional occupation of contemplatives is the development of the theological virtues.[1]

The objects of contemplation, the essential concerns of the contemplative life, are the eternal reality, the divine Persons, as well as Our Lord and the events of his life, including the Blessed Virgin—these latter being considered not merely as historical facts but as having eternal value. The contemplative life is one completely centered around eternal realities.

We should pause here to make a brief examination of conscience. When we Christians read Plato, do we not often have reason to blush? Is it only the eternal realities that count in our lives? Are the invisible realities the essential objects of our concern first, always, and above all else? Do we spontaneously take care to remain in the presence of God?

The sole preoccupation of the genuine Christian contemplative is to live in the presence of God and of the divine realities for their own sakes (not because they enrich his mind). This is what distinguishes Christian contemplation from philosophical contemplation and natural mysticism; the goal of the latter is *knowledge* of God. For the Christian contemplative, God and being with God is all that matters.

But in our religious life do we not continually come back to temporal realities? These include even the graces of God, since all that is acquired is temporal. This is why St. Teresa used to urge her nuns to be attached "not to the graces of God but to the God of grace."

Do we really try to live as children and friends of God? Is it our first reflex, for example, in connection with the things that happen in daily life, to think immediately of God? Is God our unique friend, while all other friendships are given to us by him rather than chosen by ourselves? Unless we recognize these inherent demands of the contemplative life, we are not really contemplatives.

But is it possible here on earth to live *with* the divine Persons? As long as we are on earth, can we be contemplatives in any other way than by desire? Or are there in the contemplative life certain attitudes, in line with the theological virtues, which explain why St. Augustine, for example, speaks about eternal life with such ardor that it seems to be a personal discovery of his? And when it is said that St. Dominic was always speaking either with God or about God, is this nothing but a metaphor or does it enunciate a reality? Is it really possible to live with GOD more than with our family and neighbors?

Every true Christian ranks God first *appreciatively*, as St. Thomas says—that is, as regards the value placed on God. But the question we are raising comes down to this: Are there two different types of Christian life, or only differences of degree, God being never more than the end to which all things are ordered?[2]

In other words, what *is* Christian contemplation? Is it a

theoretical and speculative knowledge acquired by study, but which has become simplified to the point of becoming a sort of repose? Is it active service of our neighbor that has become imbued with God? Or is there, in fact, an intimate knowledge of God that is more than the mere "sense of God"; a knowledge that actually puts us in God's presence? Can Our Lord love us so much that even in this world we can have a heart-to-heart relationship with him? Can God treat us as intimate friends while we are still on earth? Or, to put the question from another angle, is there a specifically Christian contemplation that is different from pagan contemplation and that appears as the great message of the New Testament?

The reply of saints and theologians is yes. This intimate knowledge of God is the fruit of the Holy Spirit's gift of wisdom. St. Thomas distinguished two types of wisdom: acquired and infused. The latter is an affective knowledge of God received as a gift; it consists essentially in an intimate relationship with God.

Wisdom is a word that lends itself to a variety of meanings. One might think that it refers only to something speculative. But, no, it refers also to a union of the heart with God, a union that is meant just as much for brothers and sisters as for priests and theologians.[3]

If God is really everything for us and if he can give us even here on earth a means of entering into intimate union with him, this intimacy will be worth more than anything else. For the Christian, this is true wisdom, the great wisdom of love, the hidden treasure, the pearl of great price.

Beatitude consists in union with God. The reason why charity takes first place in our life on earth is that it alone can bring about this union. In heaven, primacy will belong to the intellect, for there it is by means of the intellect that we will be completely united with God.

Although it has the same object as theology, infused wisdom infinitely surpasses theological knowledge as such.

The latter is, by comparison, something active. The intimate knowledge of wisdom takes place in the darkness of faith and with few explicit ideas. It requires a great poverty of spirit. (The higher forms of contemplative prayer demand even a kind of death of the intellect.)

If our primary goal is the fullness of life, we will quite naturally look to the development of our intellect. Our intellect needs enrichment; it is a faculty of appropriation. But if our primary goal is intimacy with God in love, our development will consist in the knowledge that is born of love, grows in love, and gives birth to love. In this type of knowledge, it is impossible psychologically to distinguish the act of understanding from the act of love, whereas this can always be done in the case of theoretical knowledge. In the latter case, love may, indeed, incite a person to seek knowledge; it can, for example, impel the theologian to work with greater ardor and to deepen his theology. But it is not properly love that presents the object of knowledge to him and, by the same token, his knowledge will not necessarily be followed by another act of love.

In the case of affective knowledge, however, the two acts are inseparable: knowledge is born of love and in turn causes love to grow. Love takes the place of the concept and provides the illumination. It is the act of love that puts us in contact with the object and thereby brings knowledge. Hence, the more we love, the more we know. God seems to become more and more "inaccessible to our mind but close to our heart" (St. Augustine).

In this intimate knowledge of God, we do not look so much for the lights that God can give us or even for conversation, as we do in human friendships, but simply for contact with God. It is God, our friend, whom we seek.

This intimate knowledge of God is the fruit of the gift of wisdom; the theological virtues by themselves do not suffice to produce it. This is for several reasons. We have already noted that, in the contemplative life, the theological virtues become, so to speak, our proper occupation, our professional virtues. But our human occupations and activities continue to be carried out on the plane of the moral virtues. In order to put our human life on the level of the theological virtues, so that we live the theological virtues for themselves and not merely as means to make us practice the moral virtues as God wants, the intervention of the Holy Spirit is necessary.

This intervention is necessary also because of the disparity between charity and faith. Without them, would it be possible to have friendship with someone we do not see? The gifts provide us with a contact in darkness, like the touch of a blind man.

When the good Lord makes us discover the darkness of our faith, we are inclined to fabricate images and illustrations; but this intimate knowledge annihilates all our images and introduces us into the dark core of faith and into the divine reality itself.

Knowledge of the God of wisdom necessarily plunges us into the darkness of faith. We have the peace and joy of being with God, but we are left completely in the dark because, as said above, the act of love has taken the place of a concept. If we try to grasp this presence with our minds or to know what it is, we cause this intimate knowledge to diminish. We must let ourselves be carried off in the darkness of faith. This is a kind of sleep or death of the spouse, in which we relive the death of Our Lord so that our hearts might rise again and burn with love.

Let us be deeply convinced that this intimacy with God is indeed real, even though God may not have granted it to us. Let us be contemplatives at least by desire. God grants this intimacy to whom he wills. It involves a new predilection and a new gift even for those who already have received grace

(God's first gift). Let us have the humility to acknowledge that God has not given us this gift, if that is the case, but let us never close ourselves to it.

For we can close ourselves off very quickly through a multitude of little sins against the Spirit—little involuntary sins. We must be attentive to them. According to St. Thomas, involuntary[4] sins are the least serious, because not deliberate; but their consequences can be very serious. People do not bother much about these faults against the Holy Spirit. For there is a very great freedom of spirit in the religious life, and even more in the contemplative life. We can save our souls and even lead a very perfect religious life without this intimacy with God, and even while refusing certain gifts.

But even when involuntary, these sins against the light and against the Holy Spirit have incalculable consequences. Being faithful or not to the inspirations of the Holy Spirit can affect everything in our life. Hence, the importance of an open and humble attitude of soul.

We should all ask pardon for the times we have grieved the Holy Spirit; the Blessed Virgin is the only one who never resisted the Spirit. God wants to give us gifts, and to give them in a divine way; what God wants to give us is an intimate relationship with himself. Our Lord suffered on the Cross at the sight of souls who prevented him from his divine gift of himself. (Think of the suffering we experience at the insensitivity of our friends.)

But if we have thus refused grace, let us go to the Blessed Virgin and ask her to make reparation for it. There is a reparation of love that she can bring about. That is something we can all ask for.

4

The Contemplative Life:
The Special Call of God and the
Fundamental Attitudes of the
Contemplative

We have seen that contemplation consists essentially in the affective knowledge that is the fruit of the gift of wisdom. Contemplation attains God in a different way from faith, which is a more objective[1] type of knowledge. Affective knowledge is rooted in love and blossoms into love. Love takes the place of the concept; love is its light. In this act of affective knowledge, we touch God, so to speak, and are conformed to God.

Here, knowledge cannot be separated psychologically from love; love flows into knowledge and knowledge is prolonged by love. In human friendship such a direct contact of soul with soul is not possible. But God as creator can do without representations and give himself to us directly through love. God can impart his very self to us silently in the depths of our souls.

The act of love plunges us into God, who is given in silence. Anything else would run the risk of detracting from the gift. "Silence is the speech of God," St John of the Cross says.

This act of love or affective knowledge frees us from ourselves. In heaven, our knowledge also will be ecstatic, but here on earth, love alone takes us out of ourselves.

In this love, God reveals himself to us in a silence that strips us and makes us experience that "blessed are the poor." Silence preserves us from illusion and gives us a security.

Purely theoretical knowledge is incapable of unifying and integrating us. But this affective knowledge can do so, by freeing us and stripping us of attachments. It takes away every desire of being noticed (either by others or by ourselves); it makes us love to be lost in God. The humility into which this affective knowledge plunges us is in fact one of the signs of its authenticity.

Now we must consider, first, how the contemplative life depends upon a special call from God, and second, the fundamental attitudes required of the contemplative.

CONTEMPLATION DEPENDS ON A SPECIAL CALL FROM GOD

Every vocation implies a choice, and a divine choice always stems from God's predilection, not from any merits of ours. In the case of the contemplative life, a special predilection on the part of God can be seen in the fact that God does not wait until heaven to treat us as intimate friends and communicate to us the secrets of his heart.

When we hear these words, "secrets of the heart," we tend to think in terms of information[2] or light. That is what is involved in human communication, between friends. But Our Lord can communicate his heart to us by way of love, making us conscious of his love. Such a grace is very intimate and profound, higher than graces of illumination.

Let us reflect a little on this special vocation. Are there any natural dispositions for the contemplative vocation, a vocation that imples a choice on God's part stemming from God's love? It is often said that there are, but that is completely false. In the case of a vocation to the active life, certain natural dispositions can be recognized; but for a contemplative vocation, which is the blossoming of the life of grace and of the theological virtues, there are no natural predispositions. Insofar as a call to the *religious state*[3] is involved, one may speak of the absence of counterindications; but that is all.

People sometimes speak of "mystical temperaments," meaning temperaments that are affective, artistic, which more readily adopt an attitude of openness and passivity. Do such temperaments predispose one to the supernatural life? Perhaps they make it easier to surrender to God. On the other hand, however, the "sensitivity" presupposed by the divine love, which gives rise to the intimate knowledge of contemplation, is a *divine* sensitivity, a *divine* "sense of touch." It demands immobility, perseverance, and firmness (qualities not readily found in esthetic temperaments), and even a love of darkness (whereas esthetic temperaments love light and images).

On the other hand, mathematical temperaments tend to be firm, solid, and realistic. They too have certain favorable predispositions, such as a certain firmness. When God takes hold of them, they are already stripped of sensitivity and illusions.

On the basis of experience, it cannot really be said which type the Lord more often calls to the contemplative life. God's choice quite transcends the matter of temperament and depends solely on his good pleasure. God knows well how to make the most tender hearts virile and to melt the most hardened; God acts *suaviter et fortiter*—gently and powerfully.

The grace of contemplation places the soul in a kind of immobility and silence. No human being can establish him-

self in silence; anyone who thinks he can, only shows that he
does not know anything about silence. God alone does it.
Because of the darkness of faith, we go round and round in
circles as long as God leaves us to the resources of our reason.
It is God who must immobilize us in silence. Likewise it is
God who must establish us in the present moment. This too is
something we cannot do by ourselves. God does all this by
way of love, which involves a death of the mind and a resurrec-
tion of the heart.

There is nothing therefore in our human psychology equiv-
alent to this divine knowledge. It is not a matter of temperament. We are all equally distant from it, all equally close. As a
corollary, the common life will be more difficult for contemplatives than for those engaged in the active life, since it is
the will of God alone that brings us together, not any natural
compatibility.

What, then, are the criteria by which a contemplative
vocation can be discerned? There may not be any natural
dispositions, but there are divine signs of God's predilection,
interior signs that God gives: a sense of God, a thirst for God,
a dissatisfaction with everything other than God, a sense of
the vanity of all activities, even those that are for God. There
is a sense of silence, a need of silence that is almost physical
and makes it impossible for the soul to rest anywhere but in
silence with God. These signs are all the more striking when
they occur in people of ardent and lively temperament.

Often these "touches" of God can be observed in persons
not at all predisposed toward the religious life—that is, in
converts. Furthermore, these graces of contemplative prayer
often disappear after the person enters the religious life. This
is because God wanted to show them the goal from the outset.
But God is faithful, and these graces will reappear later on,
perhaps under a different form.

Attention needs to be called to these signs during a retreat.
For just as there are involuntary faults, so also there can be

graces of which we are unaware. According to St. John of the Cross, difficulty in prayer and suffering from the absence of God are proximate signs of a call to contemplation. There are people who find it very easy to pray; but this may stem (although not necessarily) from the fact that they live in their imagination, in a sort of reverie. But if a person has a sense of what prayer is and of who God is and yet experiences difficulty in prayer, if he suffers from an intense need for it and from the certitude that God has called him to it, such a person is already engaged in contemplative prayer.

When we have the impression that we have spent our prayer time driving away distractions, but did not have recourse to meditation because meditation seemed like a duty devoid of God; when we have been left in our poverty, with nothing but this striving for God—we can be sure that God has been acting in the depths of our soul. We perceive it afterward, when we resume our other activities, by a sense of peace and rejuvenation in the depths of our heart.

At other times we may have the impression of having done much better, when it was really more superficial. But when, in our very poverty, we experience a need for God, then we can be sure of God's call.

It is important to remember the graces that God has given us in order to remind ourselves of what he expects of us. Magnanimity prompts us to do this. St. Teresa used to reproach her daughters for their lack of magnanimity more than for their lack of humility.

THE FUNDAMENTAL ATTITUDES OF THE CONTEMPLATIVE

These attitudes follow from the fact that contemplation depends upon a special call from God.

The first fundamental attitude is *fidelity*—the fidelity of the bride, the fidelity of love. We must try to be attentive or, rather, recollected (i.e., with the attention of the heart) in order to remain in the presence of God. We must seek to be present to him as directly and totally as possible, with the fewest intermediaries between him and us. This very intimate presence does not result from an effort of mind, like the presence of an idea; it is a gift of God. It consists in an affective knowledge that can be maintained even while we are engaged in other activities. It remains latent, always ready to be awakened (like the love of the bride).

Why should we thus seek to remain in the presence of God? In order to conform our wills fully to his, in order always to have the strength to discern and accomplish God's good pleasure. The goal is the *idem velle*—"willing the same thing." In order to discover God's good pleasure at each instant, we have to be in God's presence. But we cannot remain in the presence of God if we do not do his will, for this presence is not merely a presence of the mind but a presence of the heart, a presence of love. As soon as we deviate from the will of God, we abandon our contemplative life. We should look to the Blessed Virgin, the "Virgin most faithful," as our model. The fidelity of the bride says everything.

The second fundamental attitude is *confidence*—confidence in Our Lord's love of predilection for us. This should be even greater than our fidelity; for fidelity comes from us, whereas confidence relies on the fidelity of God. Our fidelity itself ought to be rooted in our confidence; and when we have not been faithful, let us rely on God's fidelity to us. We should ask ourselves whether we have always had confidence in our Lord's love. Lack of it hurts him more than anything else. Think of the sorrow we cause a friend who sees that we no longer have confidence in him.

Humility, the third fundamental attitude of the contemplative, guarantees and protects our confidence.

Humility is an invisible virtue. Yet it is the most virile of the virtues because the most metaphysical: it makes us realize that we are nothing. This is the virtue that is least recognized by the world and by philosophers; only divine love can teach it to us. It goes much farther than the virtue of religion, with which it is often confused.

Humility is the reverse side of the theological virtues, the "nothingness" that St. John of the Cross speaks about and the "self-knowledge" of St. Catherine of Siena. It is the only moral virtue that enters the sanctuary of the most divine prayer. As long as we look at ourselves, we cannot see that we are nothing. Only when God makes us aware of his infinite love can we realize that we are nothing. The angels were incapable of knowing humility until elevated to the supernatural order.

Because it is a moral virtue, however, humility remains to some degree at our disposal. If we have offended God, we can always at least humble ourselves; this fundamental attitude puts everything back into place.

"Humility," says Cajetan, "penetrates heaven." In the beatific vision humility will be total. There our act of understanding will be perfectly humbled and transported beyond itself, because it will apprehend God, not by any concept or mental word of its own, but by the Word of God.

Humility is a constant feature in the life and teaching of Catholic mystics, whereas it does not appear in natural mysticism. This is an excellent criterion.

From the practical point of view, lack of humility is the greatest hindrance to our progress. For, in order to receive a gift, we must be open; but pride closes us and hinders us from accepting any standard other than our own. This was the sin of the angels, who wanted to love God in *their* way and not according to God's standard. In this perspective, we can understand why it is said that we must undergo a kind of death and let God move us. And humility is what brings this about.

Humility was the great virtue of the Blessed Virgin, the virtue of her Immaculate Heart. Because she was immaculate, she was the only creature who was perfectly humble and who constantly grew in humility. We must ask humility of her.[4]

5

The Blessed Virgin:
Model of Our Contemplative Life

We have seen that the contemplative life is a participation in the inner life of God. It consists in an affective knowledge, a knowledge that is wholly directed to love. It is a gift of God surpassing all others. We have also seen that, since this life calls us to an activity that is, properly speaking, divine and for which nothing in our nature predisposes us, it entails a special vocation and a choice that can be made by God alone.

We have considered the attitudes that this life calls for. First there is the fidelity of the bride, fidelity to the presence of God. We sense that our fidelity ought to be constant, but we see that it is full of gaps. The Blessed Virgin is the only one who remained faithful at every moment; with us there are always moments that slip away from the grasp of God. This is a source of suffering in the contemplative life and it can be very discouraging.

But there is a still more fundamental attitude: confidence, which plunges us into God's love, fidelity, and predilection for us. This attitude is deeper and much more consoling than is fidelity. In the very midst of our infidelities we encounter God's predilection, for God wants to take us back. The Blessed Virgin, who does not want to leave us to our own resources and who wants to lead us back to our contemplative life, embraces and pursues us.

The contemplative, according to St. Augustine, is "one who is loved by God." In the contemplative life it is always God who has the initiative. But in order that there be reciprocity in this friendship, we must love God as God loves us. In other words, we must let God love himself in us; we must have our Lord's own love to love him with.

If it is God who always has the initiative, our most fundamental attitude should be one of trust or confidence. The strongest temptation for a contemplative is discouragement; but for our shelter, our trust against discouragement, there is a third attitude: humility.

Too often discouragement stems from a lack of humility. We still think we are something. Humility goes deeper than repentance. It allows us to be detached even from our faults and to avoid the sterile regrets that imply resentment toward or discontent with ourselves. For, if we are not happy with ourselves, this is because we do not truly believe that we are nothing. With humility, we are not too surprised at our faults.

One thing about which we should be very sure is that, if God permits his chosen ones to fall, it is always for a greater good: to humble them. If, therefore, after a fall we immediately humble ourselves before God, we enter again into God's will and we adore the very permission that allowed us to sin. That is how far the contemplative must go.

Now let us consider the contemplative par excellence, the Blessed Virgin. If we sense that God wants our contemplative life to develop in the school of the Blessed Virgin, we should regard that as a very great grace.

The contemplative life always implies a *predilection*—a choice made by love. Mary was chosen, not merely by contrast with sinners, but even among the saints. She was set apart from the other saints in order to be their Queen and the beloved Mother of Our Lord. This predilection made everything in her life contemplative, by that *Christian* contemplation that is to be so all-embracing, as philosophical contemplation cannot.

The sign as well as the effect of this predilection is her Immaculate Conception, the creative choice of God giving her a fullness of grace. It was a free choice on the part of God, not the result of her own merits. Perhaps one of the reasons why Protestants are so opposed to this dogma is that they see the divine maternity as a function, not a predilection: as nothing more than a service, like that of apostles and priests. (It is not proper to say that the latter are predestined to their office.)

The mystery of Mary is that she was predestined to be the Mother of God from all eternity, by an eternal divine plan. She is mother, not merely in the economy of the Incarnation, but eternally. She is Mother in glory. With that in mind, we can understand how the three attitudes of the contemplative life were wonderfully realized in her.

HUMILITY

Humility was Mary's most fundamental virtue. The faults that occur even in the holiest persons are those little acts of turning in upon oneself that cause us to put ourselves forward, or to be complacent, or to indulge in self-love—all of which are faults of pride. Pride is the universal sin, found in all other faults, even in slight, involuntary ones. We always have a tendency to appropriate something to ourselves, even the most divine gifts.

If God wanted the Blessed Virgin to be immaculate, it was above all for the sake of her humility. She was humility itself; and that is why she was always faithful. In order for God to be fully active in our lives, we must be fully open; and it is humility that opens us by making us recognize our position as creatures.

But being spirit (and, hence, persons), to retain the complete openness that becomes a creature, we must realize that we are nothing. As soon as we begin to assert ourselves a little, we close ourselves to the gift of God. It is in proportion to our humility that God can love and sanctify us. The Blessed Virgin was perfectly humble and could, therefore, receive all the graces God wanted to give her. But in what did her humility consist?

It was very different from that of Peter or Mary Magdalene. She never had to exercise the virtue of repentance (although she did indeed possess it, not being impeccable de iure as Christ was, but only by grace). In us humility is always mixed with compunction and repentance. In Mary humility had an absolute simplicity. She is the only saint who never looked at herself.

Mary was the poorest of creatures ("Blessed are the poor in spirit"). She never appropriated any grace, but accepted everything as a gift; she made the most of God's gifts, not in order to enjoy them, but in order to draw closer to God. Thus, she constantly mounted higher and higher. She received all her graces without seeing them. It was in the beatific vision, in God himself, that Mary, on the day of the Assumption, discovered the marvel that God had wrought in her. Only then did she look at herself.

Humility gave her the great simplicity that stood out so clearly at the Annunciation. Her attitude was quite different from that of St. Margaret Mary, for example, who protested her unworthiness when Our Lord revealed to her the secrets of his heart. To Margaret Mary, Jesus replied, "If I had found someone more unworthy, I would have chosen her."

The Blessed Virgin's only response was, "Behold the handmaid of the Lord." Protesting our unworthiness indicates that we still believe we are something. If we are truly convinced of our own nothingness, we know there is no proportion between what we are and what God asks of us. Then, knowing that God is all-powerful, we say, "Behold the handmaid of the Lord."

Nothing simplifies us like humility. Complexity stems from trying to appear to be something. Simplicity is the work of God in us. It comes from humility that is radical and profound. Humility is likewise one of the most lovable virtues because it gives us the freedom of the children of God.

Mary's humility was also magnanimous. Her response, "Behold the handmaid of the Lord," was the response of a servant, a useless servant. But God was asking her for a divine service. Hence she had to have not merely the attitude of a servant, but also magnanimity. Likewise with us: if God asks for a divine service (as he does in the contemplative life), we must be capable of aiming at and advancing toward something great—which is the very meaning of magnanimity. The root of Mary's simplicity was a humility so deep that it could be at the same time magnanimous.

True simplicity implies not only humility and self-forgetfulness but also freedom from dissipation and fragmentation. Little children are not really simple, because they are drawn in various directions by their whims. Only the children of Mary are truly simple. Simplicity presupposes a life centered around something great: the divine good. Nothing matters for them except the will of God: this is magnanimity. But in order to have this divine magnanimity, we must be very humble, for we have to espouse the very desires of the Holy Spirit and not be content with our own human desires.

Magnanimity means that we are attached to nothing but the will of God and God's way of seeing things. No other work should be able to satisfy us, even were it organizing a congregation or founding monasteries. Nothing suffices by itself to satisfy us; we will always return to our sole concern: "Is this the will of God? Will I be able in this activity to enter into more intimate union with God?"

This magnanimous humility is what constituted Mary's

simplicity, a simplicity flowing from her poverty of spirit. The latter resulted from the fullness of grace of her Immaculate Conception. Let us ask the Blessed Virgin to give us that simplicity.

TRUST AND FIDELITY

Humility, trust, and fidelity were all bound together in Mary. Her fidelity was so contemplative that it was identical with her trust. It was the fidelity of a bride who lived always in God's predilection. Thus, it is hard to say whether it was more fidelity or trust. Mary's unique attitude was one of trust in love. At the Annunciation Mary was faithful, but she let trust dictate her response. In the mystery of her compassion, when she accepted us as her children, instead of being dismayed, she again trusted in love.

So also with us: when we are closely united with love, even while God is giving us more and more love and uniting us more closely to himself, God gives us a presentiment of the trials we will have to endure. When they actually come, we "recognize" them and undergo them not as a punishment but as a token of God's love.

That is what happened at the Cross. Mary knew well that God was leading her in the ways of love, and that divine friendship has different laws from human friendship. Her intimate union with Jesus attained its consummation there at the Cross. She did not need purification; her trials were not a punishment for sin but a token of love. God had chosen suffering to testify on earth to his love, and God was letting her share in that suffering.

It was Mary's confidence that made her faithful, and her confidence stemmed from her nothingness. The bride of God, who has no other task but love, is spontaneously inclined to self-effacement. This is the humility of the bride who naturally loves to lose herself in her beloved spouse. Love is what impels her to a joyous humility, which is completely simple and but one with love. In moments of great intimacy with God, we hardly know whether it is acts of love or acts of humility that God asks of us. In fact, it is both together: we disappear, but we disappear in God's love.

Let us ask the Blessed Virgin to enlighten us in all our questions of conscience. Let us also meditate on all her attitudes. There was always a deep intimacy between her and our Lord, but a very dark intimacy, an intimacy in faith.

The intimacy of *the Nativity* demanded of Mary a faith in the mystery of the Incarnation greater than that of anyone else. The babe she held in her arms was like every other baby, yet he was her God.

Before the Annunciation her intimacy was one of thirst. Mary yearned for the Messiah; she embodied the desire of the entire world. There was a huge disproportion between her love and her knowledge: the intensity of her charity already surpassed that of the angels and saints; yet her faith was still that of the Old Testament. She had a grace proportionate to her future motherhood, but did not yet know the mystery of the Trinity.

At the Annunciation God fulfilled that desire, by which the yearning of the whole world was recapitulated in Mary. (In our prayer, when God leaves us in thirst and darkness, there is a presence that we feel vaguely but do not actually attain.)

During his public life, Jesus was away preaching and Mary remained close to him, but only in her heart.

Finally, there was intimacy *at the Cross,* in the glorious mysteries and, after the Ascension, in the Eucharist.

In Mary we find every possible modality of the divine intimacy. Her spousal fidelity took hold of her entire life in such a way that everything became new grounds for intimacy.

6

Prayer

Prayer is the most perfect way to stay in the presence of God. For the summit to which we aspire—contemplation or the intimate knowledge of God—is a divine gift, and prayer puts us in the best disposition to receive it. Prayer is therefore the primary activity of the contemplative life. We will examine the different types of prayer that occur in the religious life in order to discern in a very practical and concrete way how to pursue the contemplative life. There are three types: prayer of petition, prayer of thanksgiving, and prayer of friendship.

But let us note at the very outset that prayer is the most difficult thing in the world for human beings. To pray is to remain face to face with the Invisible. Prayer is said to be the lifting of the soul to God. That is very hard for us because we need sensible and visible objects; hence we are always on the lookout for pretexts to diminish the place of prayer in our life.

We must, therefore, examine the resources that are to be found in the world of prayer so as to see how we might maintain the spirit of prayer—that is, the attitude of remaining present to God, in our daily lives, no matter what the stage of our spiritual life.

PRAYER OF PETITION

We must not disdain prayer of petition. It is available to everyone and is the normal prayer of every creature as such. It becomes much more necessary when the creature is raised to the supernatural order. It is the prayer that comes forth from us spontaneously as soon as we sense that we have nothing, that we are beggars. It springs, therefore, from our being poor in spirit.

In periods of dryness, we can always beg God to bring us into a more intimate relationship with himself. When we feel that we fall short of our contemplative ideal, we can always beseech God to make us contemplatives. Petition is the humblest form of prayer; but through it prayer first enters into our lives and takes hold on us most easily.

Another of its great values consists in being a means to envelop all our actions in prayer. We should never do anything without praying first, and we should remain in this spirit of prayer while we act. Thus this humble form of prayer will give a kind of contemplative mode even to our activity. St. Thomas contrasts this kind of prayer with the order given by the human reason at the origin of every action. Whereas an order is the act of one who is in full command,[1] petition expresses the attitude of a subordinate who, knowing that he acts only as a secondary cause, submits a project to his superior before undertaking it. Petition both seeks God's support to make our action efficacious, and expresses our desire to act according to God's will, to remain in his will, and to rectify our attitude if need be. It embodies submission to God, which is an excellent preparation for the contemplative life.

Prayer of petition must be very humble if it is to be ardent. In our requests we must be concerned to conform our will to God's. We must ask only for what God wants to give us; if we sense that our request is not very pleasing to God, we must abandon it. The Blessed Virgin and the saints are always heard because they always ask for what is pleasing to God.

As we become more contemplative, this prayer will simplify until finally the best petition will be little more than our simple presence. This also shows how to deal with the intentions that others recommend to our prayers. It is enough to

take them deeply to heart at the moment they are entrusted
to us; after that, our simply being present to God will constitute a petition.

This is how prayer of petition submerges the active part of
our lives in prayer. For example, it is natural to ask God for
light when we set to work, and to return to him from time to
time as we work. When we are engaged in study, this provides
a way that is more contemplative, more humble, and more
detached: instead of acquiring the truth for ourselves, we seek
it from God. The same holds true for writing letters, or for
tasks of the moral order. Some things in the religious life—
such as obedience, the common life, submission to the rule,
and the like—are too hard for us unless we pray.

This has a special application for children of Mary. Through
contemplative prayer, she teaches us how to acquire virtue.
We need to recognize that there are many things we cannot do
by ourselves; we can do them only with our Lord's help. We
lack the strength, the willpower, or the energy. No doubt a
contemplative soul is strong, but this strength comes from
God. When the Lord has taken possession of everything in
our life—our whole heart and all our energies—we must draw
our strength from him.

There are certain temptations of the devil that will conquer
us if we try to resist them on our own. We should simply go to
Our Lord without even allowing ourselves to look at the
temptation.

An excellent form of the prayer of petition is just to stay
close to Our Lord for all the souls God has entrusted to us
(and everyone we meet is to a certain extent entrusted to us).
We should ask never to be a cause of scandal to them but
always a channel of grace. We should willingly stay close to
Our Lord in silence for them. This is an excellent form of
apostolate.

PRAYER OF THANKSGIVING

Prayer of thanksgiving complements that of petition. Prayer of petition should precede all our actions; prayer of thanksgiving brings them to a close. The latter helps us to avoid an "active" mentality by making us refer everything we have done back to God instead of appropriating it to ourselves. In this way it too helps to give a contemplative character to our activity. Thanksgiving takes on a particular importance in the supernatural order. Everything received calls for gratitude and, in the domain of the supernatural, everything is a gift.

Mary is the model of this prayer of thanksgiving. She began her life in an attitude of thankfulness (for her fullness of grace) and remained in it always.[2] She teaches her children to recognize that *everything* Jesus sends us is a gift—not only those things that appear good to us but our trials as well. Mary maintained her Magnificat even at the Cross. Normally we should not ask for suffering; it is humbler simply to let ourselves be led; but when it comes, we ought to give thanks for it.

A contemplative soul, conscious that God's predilection is always prior to anything on its part, ought never to abandon this attitude of thanksgiving. Thanksgiving is a more contemplative form of prayer than is petition, lying midway between prayer of petition and prayer of friendship. It has a wide range of application: in periods of dryness we can always thank God for all that he has given us; we can thank God for the Blessed Virgin. We cannot make petitions for Mary; but we can give thanks for her.

This leads quite naturally to an attitude of adoration before the mystery of the divine transcendence, in which we thank God simply for being God and for the mystery of the Holy Trinity, as well as for the wonders of the Blessed Virgin. Thus, the prayer of thanksgiving brings us to the wholly contemplative attitude of pure praise.

Here is another form of prayer that is always at our disposal because of the active element in it. We can praise God[3] even by our actions. This is the grandeur of the liturgy: it is a disinterested action, an action performed solely for the glory of God.

We come to God with our human resources and, by glorifying God, show him that we want to draw near and enter into intimate union with him. Thus we testify that, even when left to ourselves (for contemplation can be given only by God), we do not turn to temporal things but seek to come as close as possible to God.

PRAYER OF FRIENDSHIP

Prayer of petition is the prayer of the poor; thanksgiving is the prayer of one who has been overwhelmed with gifts. But what goes on in the prayer of friendship? First of all, contact between friends. That is the reason for conversation: it allows hearts and minds to "beat as one." Services rendered do not suffice to constitute friendship; they only lead to and flow from it. The contact necessary for friendship involves speech. *Conversatio* is the Latin word for mutual exchanges between friends. This alone permits two minds to be present to each other.

But even though conversation, in its deepest sense, is the most essential element of friendship, often in fact external works and mutual services take on greater importance. This is due to our poverty as human beings: our word is not always very spiritual or true, and friends need each other's help in acquiring other goods. But friendship with God is quite different from earthly friendships. Mere contact with God is enough to sanctify us, even though the practice of virtue continues to be necessary to prove the disinterestedness of our prayer.

But how is it possible to be friends with God? Friendship demands reciprocity and dialogue; and, as we so often say, "God does not speak to me." Prayer of petition is readily understandable, but prayer of friendship?

Actually the prayer of friendship can take two forms: in one, God leaves us to ourselves; in the other, God intervenes. The desert fathers used to distinguish three ways in which God speaks to us. The first is through creation—that is, through nature. The second way is through Scripture. Revelation makes dialogue and friendship with God possible. God speaks to us not only through Scripture, but also through tradition, the liturgy, through all those involved in the magisterium of the Church, and through holy preaching. (One of the mysteries of holy preaching is that we find in it some words spoken "especially for me.")

We must read the Gospel, conscious that it is revelation. The beatific vision, which Jesus enjoyed even while on earth, enabled him to see us who live today; and his Gospel was spoken as much for us as for those who were present then. We are therefore justified in taking every word of Scripture as material for our contemplative prayer, for "conversation" with God.

We can extend this to the lives of the saints, which are like a prolongation of holy preaching. The saints share with us some of the secrets of their intimate relationship with God; we can allow them to introduce us to their divine friend.

These first two ways of God's speaking to us (by nature and by Scripture, together with all the things associated with Scripture) belong to the first form of the prayer of friendship, in which God speaks to us indirectly. There is a third and much higher way (corresponding to the second form) in which God speaks to us through the Holy Spirit, who can give himself to us in silence. This is the most divine word of God. Only God can communicate himself to his friends in silence. "Silence is the speech of God." This is a great privilege. Even from a merely human point of view, it is so difficult to put into words that which is deepest, most intimate, and profound within us; our truest encounters take place in silence.

In the beatific vision, there is no created word; God's own Word will be the principle of our knowledge. Here on earth, however, the concepts and representations we form are not adequate to the divine reality. Hence union with God can take place here only in silence. In affective knowledge, love takes the place of concepts. For every creature, silence is superior to language: language is born of the mind whereas silence is born of love. Even in the beatific vision, there will be silence.

The Word of God originates in silence and leads to silence; this is the sign that it is the Word of God. Silence that is full, nourishing, and savory is the sign under which the presence of God both hides and reveals itself to us. This silence puts us in the presence of God while keeping us in the dark, because God's presence is known only by faith. Hence, if God has given us a thirst for silence, if God gives us this silence in contemplative prayer, we must remain there and avoid everything that might jeopardize it, for that would diminish love.

The same must be said about peace—that peace "which surpasses all understanding," as St. Paul says. The most authentic sign of the presence of God is that very deep peace that is one and the same thing as this silence.

We are speaking about interior silence, which is a gift of God. We cannot produce this silence, this peace, ourselves. It is an interior and divine peace that does not of itself imply any light (although it is itself a kind of light—the light of love). It is different even from the peace of a good conscience, which is the peace of reason. It is the peace of love, the fruit of the gift of wisdom, the first effect of God's presence and of contact with God. This peace can come only from God. When we want to know whether certain lights or graces come from God, we should look to see whether they are accompanied by this peace and recollection.

We should not neglect the lights God gives us, but we must

be even more oriented toward silence and peace. We should not try to "profit" from the time of intimate prayer by looking for enlightenment.

There is also a certain interior joy, a joy so interior that it is not immediately discernible. But *peace* is the more exact term. Peace, furthermore, is more easily reconciled with suffering and trial. Sometimes the silence is like a devouring fire that burns away all that is not God, separates us from everything else, and plunges us into the desert. But under whatever form it takes, there is always peace.

Let us ask the Blessed Virgin to help us understand all this and to teach us how to use these various forms of prayer.

7

The Contemplative Life: A Mystery of Faith

Up to now, we have considered the mystery of our contemplative life insofar as it is a mystery of intimate relationship with God. Now we must consider another aspect—namely, that this life of intimacy is realized in faith. The contemplative life is not only a mystery of love and wisdom; it is also a mystery of faith. It does not enable us here on earth to go beyond the realm of faith; nor is it some sort of middle ground between the life of faith and the life of the blessed in heaven. Rather, just as it deepens our life of charity, it also deepens our life of faith.

This aspect is very important, because everything in our religious life that pertains to keeping the rule is connected with it. If one considered the contemplative life solely from the point of view of intimacy with God and interior life, it might seem as if one had only to follow the inspirations of the Holy Spirit. To save ourselves from being painfully perplexed at the actual conditions of religious life, we must consider the aspect of faith—the aspect that brings the contemplative life into contact with the Church.

Our intimacy with God develops in darkness. Because of its inherent structure, its "psychological mechanics," this intimate knowledge never goes beyond the confines of faith. The realism of love puts us into contact with God himself. (Faith also puts us into contact with the divine reality, but in and through ideas.) The gift of wisdom entails an affective knowledge of God that enables us in a sense to touch God in and by our love. But this takes place in darkness, not in glory or light. It is like a blind man's sense of touch. God is very close to our heart but inaccessible—daily more and more inaccessible—to the grasp of our intellect. Mystical knowledge brings out the darkness at the heart of mystery.

Hence, besides the demands of love and intimacy, to which the gifts of the Holy Spirit correspond, our contemplative life must also satisfy the demands of faith. This accounts for the dryness and aridity, the darkness, separation, and night, which intervene in our contemplative life.

This is a mystery that cannot be explained simply on the grounds of our sins or the need of purification. The Blessed Virgin was immaculate; her spiritual life began in the unitive state without having to pass through the purgative and illuminative ways. Yet she too experienced the trials of faith. She is the saint who had the greatest intimacy with Our Lord; yet she is also the one who suffered most from darkness; her faith was in the worst darkness of all.

If we were to consider things only from the point of view of love, we would have a hard time comprehending the hiddenness of Mary's life. Although the Queen of Saints, she was the most hidden of all saints. Our Lord never performed a miracle for her benefit nor did she herself ever perform any. (There was, to be sure, the miracle of the Annunciation, but that miracle was for us; and it was accomplished, moreover, only *after* she gave her consent.) The reason for this lack is that her faith was strong enough without miracles and doing without them increased her merit.

There are likewise many moments of darkness and separation in our lives that cannot be explained on the grounds of sin. For example, after having drawn us completely to himself, God seems to abandon us; nothing reminds us of the

divine presence any more. This does not stem merely from
the need of purification, but from the fact that the contemplative life is a mystery of faith.

There are also other reasons of an apostolic sort. To understand them, we must consider the Blessed Virgin's complementary role in Our Lord's Passion. Jesus did not experience
the sufferings involved in faith: all of his sufferings stemmed
from love. The sufferings of faith were left to the Blessed
Virgin. That was her role of compassion, of co-redemptrix.
What Jesus asked of her was to endure the sufferings peculiar
to faith.

It is striking how these trials of faith are experienced by
souls wholly devoted to the Blessed Virgin. They may experience a contemplation that is truly infused, prayer that is quite
divine, yet absolutely desolate. They have a thirst for God that
is like thirst in the desert: they are no longer aware that thirst
itself implies God's presence (for there is a kind of thirst that
brings us somewhat into his presence). Sometimes Our Lord
detaches a soul from all things and brings it to the point where
God alone counts; then he too departs. Rather, he is present
only through the conformity of the human will with his (the
essence of charity); that is all. This produces a very painful
thirst for God.

Sometimes the Blessed Virgin wants her children to share
in her sufferings for the sake of their brothers. For example,
an apostle must often humbly acknowledge that he is in-
debted to contemplative nuns for many graces. This is the
mystery of the sharing of spiritual goods, the communion of
saints, which the Blessed Virgin likes her children to live here
on earth. She withdraws the more sensible graces from some,
in order to give them to others who have greater need of
consolations and of the experience of grace. However, the
merits of the former are just as great, perhaps even greater,
than those of the latter.

There is another aspect of faith necessary to understand the sense of the contemplative life—the aspect of sacrifice. The contemplative life is, as we have seen, at one and the same time a life of intimacy with Our Lord and a life of faith. These two are on the same level, and the latter sanctifies the activity inevitable in a human life, and through sacrifice raises it to the level of contemplation.

From still another point of view, faith implies darkness. Its specific object is something unseen, something revealed by God. Faith could, of course, have been a purely interior light; revelation could have taken place by God illumining each soul directly, without any intervention of the Church. But in fact God has willed that, besides the interior illumination of each believer, the object of faith should be presented to us by a magisterium—a magisterium that is itself a mystery. Through the magisterium, articles of faith becomes dogmas.[1] It is natural, therefore, that contemplatives, inasmuch as they draw life from dogma, should live also on this mystery of the magisterium.

Thus contemplation requires, on the one hand (since it is an utterly interior life), that we be loving spouses, formed under the direct tutelage of Jesus himself; and the other hand, that we be pupils in a school, disciples of the magisterium; hence our contemplative life must develop in a society. This is *very* mysterious: God wants us in intimate relationship, which would seem to obviate any intermediary (Protestantism reasons thus, and acts according to this logic); yet this heart-to-heart intimacy has to be lived in a society of which we must be disciples.[2] This is a mystery difficult to accept. It is the "yoke of faith" of which St. Paul speaks, a veritable participation in the death of Our Lord. Our intelligence has to be crucified if it is to yield to the demands of love.

There is a yoke already in the darkness of faith itself—in the death our intellect endures passing through that darkness. But over and above that, there is imposed on us a magisterium from which we must receive the object or formulation of our

faith. No matter how maternal the Church may be, it remains
an authority—an external authority; and this can be very
hard.

In heaven there will no longer be an exterior hierarchy.
There will indeed be a society, but one that springs up naturally from within. The only hierarchy will be that of love;
hence there will be no conflict between our contemplation
and the common life. But here on earth there is this mystery
of a life that, inasmuch as it is interior and contemplative,
demands solitude, yet is obliged to develop within a society.
This sometimes leads to conflicts.

In order to appreciate the nourishment and life we derive
from the jurisdiction of the teaching Church over our minds,
we must first adopt the attitude of disciples with all the
constraints that that entails. If we fail to recognize this aspect
of faith and of the church, we religious will be tempted to
embrace only those things that enrich or foster our interior
life and to let the rest go—to ignore, for example, the role of
sacrifice in our lives.

Thus, the liturgical life can, at times, seem very burden-
some, especially when Our Lord draws us into a more silent
kind of union with him. What are we to do at times like these?
We should make the sacrifice of obedience and abandon ourselves to the Blessed Virgin, who can reconcile everything.

This attitude of obedience is connected with faith. Love
makes us accept the demands of obedience, but it is faith that
explains the obedience we owe. If we considered things solely
from the point of view of love, obedience to the inspirations of
the Holy Spirit would suffice. The obedience required by our
religious life can be understood only in the light of faith and
by the fact that faith is given to us in and through the Church.
For Our Lord has inspired the Church to organize the life of
the evangelical counsels, not according to our individual
needs, but according to a rule. Life under a rule presupposes
an attitude of faith.

Many young people hang back from the religious life for fear that too rigid a framework would check the *élan* of their contemplation. But in fact, it is the "regular" life, the common life, that has proven historically to be the most conducive to the development of the contemplative life. Christian contemplation—divine contemplation—demands charity, but charity requires the development and practice of all the virtues. This is where the contemplative life differs from the intellectual or esthetic life. The latter demand certain virtues but not all.

Docility to the Holy Spirit requires complete detachment from ourselves. The great danger of the mystical life is that, for want of discernment, we take our caprices or esthetic intuitions (which do indeed dispose us toward natural mysticism) for inspirations of the Holy Spirit. The greatness of the religious life comes from the fact that it keeps us in a state of constant renunciation of our own will by means of the seal of obedience. Hence, this common life, in which caprices and fantasies are suppressed, and all external relations regulated by obedience in order to strip and purify us, is in the long run the best school for preparing us to be led by the Holy Spirit and the best state for allowing the Holy Spirit complete freedom in our lives.

The work of the Holy Spirit is essentially interior; obedience bears directly on external acts and objects. Hence they can be reconciled very harmoniously: the Holy Spirit has all the more freedom in our interior lives in proportion as we have fewer preoccupations in our exterior lives. Once everything has been placed lovingly under the seal of obedience— an obedience willingly and lovingly accepted—the life of love can very well be reconciled with almost any activity.

Furthermore, the regular life binds us more strongly to the Church—a fact that gives us all the more security.

When we have difficulties in regard to faith (and difficulties in the religious life are always, at bottom, difficulties of faith), we should have recourse particularly to the Blessed Virgin. We should also recall the assurance given by Our Lord: "Blessed are those who have not seen but yet believe" (John 20:29).

Faith means merit. If charity is fire, faith supplies the fuel. Difficulties with obedience generally stem, not from obedience as such, but from faith; they are basically difficulties of faith.

Think of the finding of the child Jesus in the Temple (Luke 2:41–51). Jesus had disappeared. Mary looked for him in desolation and anguish. When she finally found him, he asked her, "Why were you looking for me?" At first sight we might be tempted to take this to mean that the Blessed Virgin was somehow in the wrong for following her maternal instinct and that Our Lord was reproaching her for it. But, given the fact of her Immaculate Conception, this could not be the case. Mary never committed a fault nor had even the slightest inclination to do so. In everything she did, she acted under the inspiration of the Holy Spirit. We cannot suppose that she was unfaithful to her contemplative life for three whole days! It had to be the Holy Spirit who inspired her to look for Jesus.

The Gospel adds, "They did not understand what he said to them." That was because they were confronted with a mystery—a mystery of faith. Such conflicts were continually recurring in Mary's life.

This scene contains many examples for our religious life. We may do something out of an interior inspiration and suddenly find ourselves up against the opposition of a spiritual director or superior. We are thus confronted with two "wills of God" that seem to be mutually opposed. Must we say that there has to be error on one side or the other? That will be our answer if we insist absolutely on having an explanation, on being able to understand; for there does indeed seem to be a contradiction between these two "wills."

But if we accept the mystery of these "partial" wills of God that appear contradictory, we will let God reconcile every-thing by placing ourselves very simply under obedience. The mystery of God's will is greater than we think; it goes far beyond our understanding. It belongs to the mystery of God's transcendence. If Mary and Joseph "did not understand," this was for the greater merit of their faith.

Mary was not upset by what Jesus said to her. She mar-veled, of course, at the mystery of her son, which was proving to be even greater than she had realized; but her role as mother continued as it had been. "He was subject to them": their life was not interrupted or unsettled by this event.

We need not be surprised, then, at certain apparent con-flicts. Our life is far more mysterious than we realize. The demands of love and of faith make themselves felt simulta-neously. But God is above these divisions, communicating himself to us in faith as well as in love. We should adopt a very practical attitude and ask, "What does God want of me here and now?" We should not try to see farther ahead; otherwise we run the risk of aborting some plan of God to be revealed only later on.

It is good to think often of the finding of Jesus in the Temple, and let our lives be illumined by it.

8

Hope and Difficulties
of the Contemplative Life

We have seen that our contemplative life is a mystery of both light and darkness. To avoid being disoriented by the paths on which God leads us, and to discover the guiding plan, interior as well as exterior, of our contemplative lives, we must be attentive to the implications of both love (gifts of the Holy Spirit, intimacy with God) and faith (aridities, separation from God, waiting for God, etc.). The contemplative life is at once a mystery of life and of death. There is death in our oblation—the "sacrifice" of our vows; there is life wherever there is love.

One of the most painful and disturbing aspects of the contemplative life is its lack of continuity. The need for unity amid great complexity (apostolic life, intellectual life, liturgical prayer, contemplative prayer, etc.) is, moreover, characteristic of the Dominican life. The problem presents itself differently for each of us.

We would like to create unity in our lives,[1] but if we attempt this too grossly and humanly,[2] we expose ourselves to failure. The only unity possible here on earth is the profound unity deriving from our effort to remain constantly under the movement of the Holy Spirit—that is, to live in the present moment, conformed to God's good pleasure.

This is especially true for the friars. The unity of their apostolic life does not derive from the various contributions they make (on the contrary, these tend to create diversity) but from their attitude toward God. It is the movement coming from God, not from those to whom they minister, that unites them.

The more our contemplative life develops, the more we find ourselves passing from moments of light and intimacy with God to terrible moments in which there is nothing but faith to hang onto. The farther we advance, the more the half-tones disappear, giving place to painful alternations between life and death, heat and cold. It may be that we have never felt our hearts so cold since entering religious life. Perhaps there will even be moments when we think that we scarcely have any faith left.

The trials of faith experienced by contemplatives sometimes exhibit psychological symptoms similar to those of tormented unbelievers. God, wishing to treat us as friends, strips our faith of all the human supports it might find in our families (if they are Christian) and in our tradition. God carries out these purifications in every interior soul for the merit of its faith, for its role in redemption, and in order that it might know the trials of unbelievers.

Faith by its essence implies a certain consciousness, but a consciousness *in faith,* not a psychological consciousness. The latter, in fact, must be transcended. This is why the acts of our contemplative life appear to be so discontinuous. God strips us of all those reverberations of faith in our psychology, which are distinct from faith itself. God wills to suppress all the human context that enveloped our faith as a kind of psychological incarnation of it, but on which, to a certain extent, we let our hope rest.

This discontinuity is characteristic of the contemplative life. Cultural riches provide a certain security and continuity. We are always able to utilize them; they are at our disposal. For example, theologians have possession of their theology even when they are not using it; they *can* when they want to.

But in the contemplative life nothing is acquired; the essential reality is a gift of God and it alone has value for us. By the same token, we have no security: when God is present, we are like the apostles on Mt. Tabor; when he is not, we experience anguish we would never have known in ordinary life.

Hence, the continuity of our contemplative life, amid these alternations between life and death, cannot come from light, but only from love stripped to its bare essentials: *idem velle*, conformity to the divine good pleasure. There are moments when God chooses to foster our life of love, and others when God sees fit to make us live intensely according to the demands of faith.

Insofar as they pertain to the very nature of faith, these trials were experienced by the Blessed Virgin. In us, however, they are frequently due to the need for purification. After drawing us close, God often plunges us into aridity, perhaps because of some little infidelity. We then have the painful awareness of being at fault, and the knowledge that we are being punished hurts very much. But we must realize that, while God takes the occasion of our infidelities to withdraw from us and so teach us humility, these moments of aridity are in any case necessary for our contemplative life. We must not linger too long in an attitude of regret; rather we should humble ourselves immediately, and joyfully welcome the opportunity of giving God a proof of our fidelity.

THE ROLE OF HOPE

According to St. Thomas, hope derives from the fact that here on earth charity must develop in faith. We are called to live a life of friendship with God, and friendship demands presence. But we live under the regime of faith, which implies a certain absence, at least as regards the mind. Our contact with God is not intellectual but affective, and so hidden from the mind.

How can this essentially spiritual friendship, which demands total presence, develop in faith? It can do so through hope, which implies both desire and promise. The soul will not really be the bride of Christ until heaven; here on earth its situation is more like that of a fiancée. Our friendship with God on earth is only a foretaste of what awaits us. Thus, hope, the attitude of the wayfarer, plays an essential and immensely important role for contemplatives, who sense much more keenly than others that they are exiles and prisoners on earth.

Hence also everyone in this community should be a contemplative at least in desire, recognizing that this is our vocation. Even though the graces of contemplation are given as God sees fit, everyone here can and should look forward expectantly to the fulfillment of God's promise. Like a faithful fiancée, refusing to be interested in anything except the coming of her bridegroom, we keep our hearts completely free for God.

Like magnanimity, this attitude of hope takes on a particular coloring in the contemplative life through the influence of the gifts of the Holy Spirit: it turns into confidence. A contemplative does not hope for God's help as if God were merely an omnipotent benefactor. Our Lord has already shown himself to be a friend; he has given tokens of his friendship. Hence, the contemplative's hope is an attitude of confidence in a friend who has already proven himself.

This sort of confidence develops into what is called abandonment. Hope is not merely strong desire; it must also include a firm tending toward a goal. God is the goal of theological hope, which is the virtue of one who knows that what he wants is hard to attain, and who expects the help of

one stronger than he in order to surmount the difficulty. (St.
Thomas situated hope in what he calls the "irascible ap-
petite," which has to do with reaction to difficulty.) The gifts of
the Holy Spirit add to hope a delicate note of waiting on God.
Having put our trust in him, we await his moment. This form
of hope, less active in character than the more ordinary form,
is what is called abandonment.

MARY, MODEL OF OUR HOPE

The contemplative life in itself is quite simple, involving
neither questions nor problems. Indeed, a life that consists
essentially in the theological virtues, and in which one has
only to follow the will of God from moment to moment,
should normally have a very simple line of development. To
what extent, then, can we speak of struggles and crises in the
contemplative life? And on what level do they take place?

Let us consider the Blessed Virgin, who is a model not only
of faith but also of hope. Confidence reigned in her life; she
did not have an anxiety-ridden temperament. She did, however, live in faith, and faith always implies at least the sem-
blance of struggle.

In considering the mystery of the finding of the child Jesus
in the temple, we saw the apparent conflict between two
different wills of God. There are antinomies between the
demands of nature and the demands of grace. At the cross,
Jesus asked Mary to participate in his friendship for Judas,
and to take us as her children at the very moment she saw our
sins crucifying him. There the opposition between nature and
grace was at its peak.

But was there a struggle? Only in the sense that the elements that make for a struggle were there, as can be seen from
the angel's words, "do not be afraid . . ." or from Mary's

words, "We sought you sorrowing."[3] These were the occasion of merit, but Mary always remained docile to the Holy Spirit. The unique law of her life was God's good pleasure; she always yielded to him. And if one of the opponents in a contest surrenders, we cannot really say there was a struggle.

Consider also her conduct with regard to St. Joseph. God wanted Mary and Joseph to live a common life of great intimacy. They shared the same secret calling to a virginal life. But after the Annunciation—an event that had a direct bearing on their marriage—God seems to have required Mary to keep silence about the origin of her pregnancy. This threatened to disrupt their common life. Even more perplexing is the fact that, while Mary was visiting Elizabeth, who was only a distant cousin, God himself broke the silence by revealing the secret to Elizabeth. Here we see clearly that it is God's good pleasure to reveal his secrets to whom he will, and not to those who normally would be expected to know them.

Moreover, at the Annunciation, Mary had to believe on the word of an angel, whereas at Sinai God himself spoke to Moses. God used an intermediary when calling her to this intimately personal relationship as his mother. Such antinomies were continually recurring in Mary's life. But there were, strictly speaking, no struggles or crises in the sense of two adversaries each maintaining their own position. There were moments of terror on the surface of Mary's soul, but the profound law of her life was God's good pleasure, which made everything simple.

We need not be surprised, then, to find in our own contemplative lives the elements of struggle and even—since we are not pure like Mary—actual struggles. These are the initial impulses of our minds, dismayed at two apparently contradictory wills of God; but as soon as we determine where God's will really lies, we must surrender to it. Let us ask Mary to help us with this; we must never willingly struggle with God. It is very sweet to surrender to God, but also very difficult. It

requires total renunciation of our intellect and reason,[4] and
that we become like little children. This is a grace we must
pray for.

We must be very careful because the devil often tempts us
to play with the grace of God. He urges us not to yield
immediately, under the subtle pretext of wanting to analyze
the matter and weigh the pros and cons. But this is at bottom
the attitude of an adult, not of a child. It is neither very loyal
nor very pure; it is not the attitude of love. Whenever we
sense that we are toying with God's grace, we should ask God
to purify us of this extremely dangerous and tactless fault. We
should tell God in advance that we always want to be overcome by him. Let us ask Mary to make this our fundamental
attitude.

9

The Sacraments and the Contemplative Life

The contemplative life is a mystery of both intimacy and darkness, in which God comes closer and closer to our heart, but more transcendent and inaccessible to our mind. Of itself, a contemplative life is one of silence and solitude. But since it is carried on in faith, and since God wills that the object of faith be presented to us by the magisterium of the Church, the contemplative life needs to develop within the bosom of the Church.

It is therefore important to consider the means that the Church gives us for growing in our contemplative life. There is a wide range of them. Without lingering over the more external ones, employed for all the faithful, we will focus our attention on the two great ones, which grow in importance as we advance in the contemplative life: preaching and the sacraments. These are the essential means established by Our Lord himself for the development of the life of grace in us; and the contemplative life is nothing other than the life of grace.

The sacraments are more than simple liturgy.[1] They are efficacious signs established, not by the Church, but by Christ himself. St. Thomas does not class them with the ceremonial precepts of the Old Law but on the level of grace, therefore on the same plane as the theological virtues. Hence, in preparing to receive the sacraments well, it is not enough to adopt an attitude of worship; this regards the sacrament only as an exterior rite. To profit fully from the sacraments, we need to make acts of faith, hope, and love. This applies not only to the Eucharist but also to the Sacrament of Reconciliation and all the sacraments.

The reality signified by the sacraments is grace. This is why the sacraments have an extremely important role in the contemplative religious life, in which the great problem is to reconcile intimacy with God and life in community. The sacraments are bonds or junctions given by God to link our exterior and interior life.

Let us see this in the case of the Eucharist. Liturgy is what gives our life its grandeur, and since the liturgy is essentially eucharistic, our life is centered on the Eucharist.[2] Exteriorly, life is measured by space and time. So far as space is concerned, the chapel, with the presence of the Eucharist, is what distinguishes a monastery or convent from an ordinary house. In this respect, Eucharist is the center and soul of a religious house. So far as time is concerned, the liturgy punctuates our time and gives it a sacred rhythm, centered on the Mass. Thus the mystery of the Eucharist creates a unity between the exterior and interior aspects of our life.

Authentic Christian spirituality, no matter what particular form it takes, always hinges on the sacraments. The schools of spirituality inspired by St. Ignatius give a very great place to the Eucharist and to the Sacrament of Reconciliation, as well as to spiritual direction, which is closely connected with the latter. The same is basically true of the Carmelites; yet liturgy as such has a minor role to play for both of them. *Every* contemplative needs the sacraments as well as the preached Word of God. The need for liturgy, on the other hand, varies with the times and spiritualities as well as with individual vocations and dispositions.

THE EUCHARIST

The Eucharist is the dearest sacrament for the contemplative; it is *the* sacrament of contemplation, for it is the sacrament of unity. Jesus' discourse at the Last Supper is the charter of the contemplative life, and this discourse was preceded by the institution of the Eucharist. It is striking that Our Lord waited until that moment to say what he did, as if he wanted first to give his Apostles this sign of his love so that they might be better able to understand and enter into the contemplative life. It is also striking that this message is delivered to us by St. John, the one most intimately bound to Jesus by love, and the closest to him at the moment of institution of the Eucharist, when his head rested on Our Lord's heart.

Our Lord instituted this sacrament especially for contemplatives. It is the sacrament of eternal life; and the contemplative life *is* eternal life. The Eucharist is a great support for our contemplative life. Even though, like the other sacraments, it is a sacrament of faith, it is also a sacrament of love and union.

The Eucharist is also an effective support for us amid the difficulties deriving from the fact that the contemplative life is one of intimacy lived in darkness, of charity lived in faith. The Eucharist is Jesus himself come to help us. We often experience this, although this does not necessarily mean that our sense of unity with him is strongest at the moment we receive the sacrament. (This last point need not surprise us, because sacraments are also professions of faith. It is quite possible that what God wants above all from us at the moment of receiving him is acts of faith.) But we can be certain that the Eucharist brings us graces of intimate union with Our Lord, and that without it our contemplative life would diminish.

According to Cajetan, the contemplative life is "that which

is finest in the Church." Hence, it is natural to suppose that, in instituting the Eucharist, Jesus had his contemplatives especially in mind. It is the sacrament of friendship and presence, in which he gives himself to us and wants to become one with us.

This defines the role of contemplatives. So many of the faithful approach this sacrament without an attitude of friendship. Contemplatives ought therefore to receive the Eucharist, but for others, for the whole Church, not just for themselves. They need to become souls whose inner disposition corresponds in some measure to what this sacrament signifies and demands. Jesus himself, the author of grace, is given to us here; all the potentialities of grace ought therefore to be realized in contemplatives, who are like the guardians of the Eucharist.

We should also love to receive the Eucharist for those who are far from Our Lord. We communicate not only with Jesus but also with the Church.

Is there a properly contemplative way to receive Communion?

In instituting the Eucharist, Our Lord was thinking not only of his Church, his Apostles, and his contemplatives; but above all of his mother. The Blessed Virgin's life on earth after the Ascension is a very great mystery. It would seem as though she ought by rights to have been taken away with Jesus, apart from whom the world had no meaning for her.[3] Why, then, was she kept here? No doubt, it was in part for us and for the Church; but it was for her own sake also, that she might become even more beautiful and holy.

This last phase of Mary's life was a eucharistic phase. If Mary had been the only person in the world, the sacraments, insofar as they are remedies for sin, would not have been necessary, for she was immaculate.[4] But since she had to watch over the beginnings of the Church, it was only normal that she live by its mysteries and, hence, by the sacraments.

Obviously there were some sacraments that she did not need to receive; but the Eucharist was her sacrament par excellence, because it was the sacrament of the Body and Blood of Jesus.

Since Jesus had chosen her to be our mother, and since he loved her more than all the rest of Church together, he must have instituted the Eucharist above all for her. She is the one who needed him most.

During this last phase of her life, not only was Mary's charity fully developed, but her faith also had its supreme exercise. She had to believe not only in the divinity of Jesus, as when he was physically present, but also in his humanity in the Eucharist. Moreover, there was a painful gap between her faith and her charity. Mary loved Jesus, her God, with a mother's love. "The divine mother," the saints have dared to call her. And her motherhood did not end on earth; she was predestined to remain his mother in glory. Deprived of the physical presence of Jesus, she was plunged more deeply than ever before into the darkness of faith. This made her the poorest, the most mendicant of all the saints. Her need for Jesus in the Eucharist was almost physical; the Eucharist was a true viaticum[5] enabling her to go on living.

This also shows us the special affection that the Blessed Virgin had for the priesthood. She was not a priest herself. She was not able to make Jesus present in the sacraments. She needed a priest, not to give her Our Lord's words, but for the Eucharist; and for her that was a truly vital need. She must have looked upon the Apostles as a beggar looks upon a benefactor.

Let us ask Mary to give us that same hunger for the Eucharist that she had. If we aspire to be apostles, this hunger is the best witness we can give. In our communions and in our adoration of the Blessed Sacrament, let us ask her to give us some of her longing for the real presence of Our Lord and some of her awareness that Jesus in the Eucharist is the great exterior support of our contemplative life (exterior inasmuch as a sacrament is a sensible sign).

The Eucharist is indeed food, a food given to us in the context of a sacrifice in order that we might live by that sacrifice. Jesus willed that the Eucharist not be separated from the Mass, in order that we might live from his sacrifice. Thus, the Eucharist is the unique means of reconciling the two aspects of intimacy and sacrifice in a contemplative life. The whole active side of our life should, in fact, take on the aspect of sacrifice. Our vows themselves are a sacrificial oblation.

The last phase of Mary's life remained entirely in the light of the mystery of her compassion. At each Mass she renewed her sacrifice to God and her acceptance of the state of separation in which she was living. We should learn from her to unify our religious life around the Eucharist; for the chief sacrifice of our contemplative life lies in the separation and the faith that it involves.

Even the greatest saints were not able to exhaust all the virtualities of the Eucharist. None of them ever lived completely the intimate relationship it implies. Only the Blessed Virgin succeeded in realizing its potential to the degree that a creature can. She was a "worthy mother" because immaculate. May she teach us how to receive Holy Communion somewhat as she did. May she increase our faith and charity. Perhaps Our Lord will allow us to discover through the Eucharist something of his intimacy with her.

10

The Liturgy

The Eucharist is, as we have seen, the great sacrament of the contemplative life. In it Our Lord himself comes to help us unify our lives. The Eucharist enables us to reconcile the demands of love and faith, and thus serves as the sacrament and means of unity amid the discontinuity of our contemplative life. But it is also the sacrament of faith: it has been given to us because, walking in faith, we need signs. It enables us to refocus our lives on the invisible reality that ought to be much more real for us than the exterior realities among which we live. It is good to receive Communion to show Our Lord that we believe in our contemplative life. This is something we can always do, no matter what dryness or aridity we might be experiencing.

We have seen the importance of the interior signs of a call to the contemplative life that God gives us. The Eucharist is an exterior sign given to everyone, to which we can always have recourse. It reminds us how far God's predilection has gone; in it our Friend comes to dwell among us. He takes on the form of food to show us his desire to be with us every day. He assumes the appearance of bread because it is the simplest and most common food. If he had wanted to manifest his greatness, he would have chosen a more precious material; but love is what he wanted to show. Hence he used bread, an everyday food, the nourishment of the poor.

Whenever we receive Communion, let us ask Our Lord to strengthen our faith in his predilection for us and in our contemplative life. This life is bound up with the Eucharist. The very theology of the Eucharist demonstrates Jesus' desire for contemplative souls. The fact that he wishes to remain with us in this way evidences his desire for an intimate relationship with us.

Being both sacrament of unity and a sacrifice, the Eucharist enables us to unite the two aspects of our life: contemplation or intimacy, and the aspect of sacrifice. Jesus saved the world by an act, a sacrifice. It is by sharing in that sacrifice that we will gain the strength to unify these two summits of our life and thereby bring this life to its fulfillment.

The Eucharist also unites the interior contemplative life, in which God is given in the silence and secrecy of our souls, and the exterior life—that which we live in community. For the Eucharist is, on the one hand, an efficacious sign of actual intimacy with Our Lord as well as of the still more intimate relationship that is yet to come both here on earth and in heaven. On the other hand, this sign is given to us at the altar table and during the common banquet, the great community action of the day.

The Eucharist is the sacrament of unity for apostles too. It is the beginning and the end, the starting point and the crown of their life of interior union with Our Lord, while at the same time the takeoff point for their apostolic life. They offer Mass for the people they are about to approach: they receive Communion for those who do not receive it themselves and who cannot be approached. Conscious of the fact that the priesthood is for the sake of the Eucharist, they never cease trying to lead souls to the Eucharist.

To understand the full significance of the Eucharist we must take up the liturgy and its place in our life. But in order to treat the liturgy in a truly theological and contemplative manner, we must view it in light of the Eucharist. For there is always a danger of taking a merely historical point of view, seeing only the exterior rites, which constitute the generic element of every religion. But the mystery of our Christian liturgy consists in the fact that these exterior rites are ordered to the sacraments and thereby to grace. Far from having a merely symbolic value, the liturgy gets its grandeur from the fact that Jesus is present there. That is why the liturgy is a mystery: it presents Jesus in the various events of his life, events that are themselves mysteries.

Because of its human grandeur, we run the risk of failing to look at the liturgy in a sufficiently theological and contemplative way—which is, however, the only way to make it live. The liturgy involves ceremony; and by the virtue of religion, by obedience, and in witness to our faith, we are obliged to observe carefully a protocol established by the Church. It would be wrong to omit it, look down upon it, or take from it only those elements that favor contemplative prayer; for it is the Church, the Bride of Christ, that gives us these rubrics. But it would be an equally grave error to see in the liturgy only the rites and, while carefully observing them, to neglect the theological virtues, without which liturgy has no life. A certain conformity to and love of tradition is, therefore, necessary. But we must always remember that the exterior rites exist for the sake of interior worship.

THE MYSTERY OF THE LITURGY

Let us consider briefly this mystery of the liturgy. Even though the sacraments are its chief moments, we can distinguish liturgy as such from the sacraments. (We make the distinction, of course, only in view of uniting the two all the more intimately.)

Sacraments are efficacious signs established ultimately by

Our Lord himself. They are found in both the East and the
West: they are universal. Liturgy, however, varies from place
to place; and the Church holds tenaciously to this diversity of
rites, which is one of its riches. In establishing the New Law,
Our Lord did not lay down any ceremonial precepts; he left
that to the Church. He did, however, establish the sacraments, which are far more important than the exterior rites.[1]

Because of their universality the sacraments are marked by
a certain simplicity and poverty—the poverty of the Gospel
(think of a Mass celebrated in a concentration camp). The
liturgy is like a splendid garment with which the spouse of
Jesus covers over the poverty of the sacraments, making use of
a whole ensemble of symbols. The Church thus shows itself to
be an incomparable teacher. It is a bride who, to honor her
spouse, draws attention to the gems he has given her by
displaying them as splendidly as possible. This shows not only
the grandeur of the liturgy but also its relativity. We must take
care that the garments, which ought to highlight the sacraments, do not, by their richness, conceal the treasure they are
meant to display. It is important to make full use of these
riches, but still more important to maintain their right orien-
tation and give them their proper direction.

What are these riches? In the liturgy the church provides a
framework, a milieu—partly spiritual, partly temporal—for
our contemplative life. The latter, as we have seen, involves a
certain discontinuity. The Lord makes us experience our poverty of spirit acutely; we therefore feel weak and awkward. He
asks us simply to remain in his presence, thus doing away with
all the intermediaries and human supports that might give
stability to our contemplative life. He does this to make us
rely on him alone.

Here the Church in its maternal kindness provides the
framework of liturgical and religious life as a help. It surrounds
us and protects us as much as possible with the sacred.

Thus the cloister, the enclosure within which we work, is a

sacred place blessed by the Church. And this is not for
nothing. We must respect the cloister, for there is a grace to
be found in it. It is "the King's garden." Working there is not
the same as going to work outside.

Likewise the religious habit is blessed. Its formal lines give
it the character of a sign; it represents the protection with
which the church envelops us. The religious life is meant to
embrace everything in us; and the Church in its maternal
goodness strives to sanctify everything, knowing that our contemplative life can be diminished by so many factors in our
exterior life.

That is why, even within the sacred enclosure itself, there
are oases of silence—that is, special places in which exterior
silence is observed more strictly. There may be times when
we suffer from a lack of interior silence; at least we can show
good will and a thirst for silence by doing our best to observe
it exteriorly, in the spirit of the liturgy, even if it be only the
silence of activity. Our Lord may be imparting his presence at
any given moment to some of our sisters or brothers; by
keeping silence ourselves, we at least show him our respect.

Thus this framework will give a certain continuity to our
contemplative life by shedding its light on the active part of
our life, as well as by prolonging and recalling the blessed
moments of contemplation.

We can go even further and say that the liturgy provides not
only an exterior framework for us as a community, but also an
individual framework for each one. In an external way, it
sanctifies the life of our senses. Here again we see the goodness and the prudence of the Church; rather than provoking
our sensibility by repressing it, the Church seeks to sanctify it
and turn it back to God. The Church permits the body to have
its own part in prayer, thus disposing us for interior worship
and, by the same token, allowing our interior worship to
irradiate our body. And in order that this influence might
remain hidden, that it might be exercised without betraying

"the King's secret,"[2] it is channeled by a protocol.

This is one of the wonders of Catholic worship. The exterior signs, and the chant sung by all together, give us a discrete communion with one another. The soul puts all its fervor and ardor into the liturgy; but these remain hidden under the rubrics.

This leads to another aspect of the liturgy: exterior worship is a beginning of the communion of saints. We should come to the divine office concerned above all to remain united with God; this is the "attention" that is most indispensable. But each one's contemplation, love, and union with God are contributed to the common fund.

It is one of the grandeurs of Gregorian chant to let us be active on two fronts: remaining in the presence of God, intimately united with God, and at the same time sharing with others through the chant. Hence, it is not enough to be concerned with the beauty of the singing; we should be concerned also about recollection and charity toward others. We bring our prayer and fervor to them, thus avoiding excessive individualism in our contemplative life. That would imply an attitude of self-appropriation that would no longer be divine.

Thus the liturgy can become an important factor in the common life. Difficulties and petty disagreements can occur in any community and it is not always possible to give explanations or repair discords. But when we meet together in choir (or in the refectory), the silence and common prayer can powerfully restore our friendships. We experience the joy of being once again one in heart and soul, the joy of harmonizing our intelligence, our heart, and even our voice with those of others. The really great exercises of the common life do not take place in the recreation room but in the choir and refectory. Indeed, there is no greater exercise of common life than prayer together.

Let us hold fast to these bonds of our contemplative life.

One who has received certain talents from God should come to choir with an affection for the others, which would give him the joy of sharing this gift with them through the singing. One not so endowed should come with an open heart and with the desire to receive from the others. In either case we must never have a closed, "ivory tower" attitude but should keep our hearts open and free.

We should come with the conscious intention of exercising our common life. Each one's graces are different; the good Lord does not lead all souls by the same path. Our sharing in one another's particular graces constitutes the grandeur of the office that we say together. Openness implies humility—the humility of opening ourselves interiorly to all the sources of living water around us.

We should come to choir, then, with a twofold attitude: (1) love for God and for the brothers and sisters with whom we are to share our gift, and (2) humility that is open to receive from them. We all have to receive from one another.

Finally, the liturgy has an apostolic character. This is its maternal role of creating a milieu for others, of surrounding them with prayer. In this sense, the liturgy is the great apostolic moment of the monastic life.

Let us ask Mary to give us an immense love for the liturgy, and to teach us to understand and to live it.

11

Holy Preaching

Along with the Eucharist and the liturgy, holy preaching[1] is given to us by the Church as one of the means most directly adapted to the contemplative life. Just as the eucharist is the great sacrament of the comtemplative life, so too, among the various apostolic activities confided to the Church by Our Lord, holy preaching is *the* essential function, the one that Jesus himself practiced, the one to which all the others are ordered, and the one that best corresponds to the contemplative life.

The Church encourages apostolic movements, study groups, public lectures, and the like; but these things have no place in the cloister. They are not directly *doctrinal*. They are all connected with teaching, but simply as a human enterprise. They do not directly address faith as such, nor require of the hearer, as holy preaching does, the attitude of a disciple. They are useful for those who would not otherwise be reached by the doctrine of Christ, but that is a different matter from the contemplative life.

There are, moreover, various forms of preaching, among which that which we call *holy preaching* is the most directly ordered to the purely contemplative life. *Apologetic preaching* is addressed primarily to reason; it tries to draw people to the faith. Holy preaching is aimed primarily at engendering, nourishing, and developing a faith already present. Hence, apologetic preaching does not belong in the cloister. When contemplatives have difficulties with faith, the best way to overcome them is not by reasoning but by developing their faith through growth in love.

Neither is *catechetical preaching* appropriate for contemplatives—not even for recent converts who have but a poor knowledge of the faith. According to St. Thomas, catechetical preaching is the task of pastors and priests insofar as they are ministers of the sacraments: it provides the rudiments of the faith necessary for the worthy reception of the sacraments.

Moral preaching teaches how to live a Christian life in the midst of the world, how to keep our moral life on a level with our supernatural life, how to live in the world according to the demands of faith.

Holy preaching, on the contrary, unveils the mysteries that are the objects of the faith; and it presents them as the nourishment of our faith. Contemplatives live from the mysteries of the faith, and holy preaching provides them with their proper nourishment. Hence it is addressed most especially to them and is essential for them.[2] It is likewise the function of holy preaching to propose the ideal of Christian perfection and how to live according to the evangelical counsels. It presupposes that the preacher himself have an experience of contemplation.[3]

Holy preaching is a divine function, more so than the academic teaching of theology. The latter may be superior, in a certain sense, to the extent that it aims at the formation of clerics and future preachers; nevertheless, theologians as such do not pertain to the teaching Church but to the Church being taught. Holy preaching is divine because its role is simply to present the divine mysteries, the mysteries of the faith. This cannot take place unless God uses the preacher as an instrument. Holy preaching is a gift of God, just as much as is contemplation, and the preacher is God's envoy. We can prepare ourselves for this work, but we cannot "learn" how to do it any more than we can learn how to be a good confessor. There is something charismatic about it. One can get oneself ready, but it is God who must use the instrument. It is, therefore, completely false to treat preaching as a popularization of theology. Holy preaching is a divine mystery—the mystery of Jesus still living and preaching in his Church.

Mary, the contemplative par excellence, profited fully from holy preaching. For three years her contemplative life was nourished by the preaching of Our Lord himself; the Gospels let us suppose that she was in the crowds that listened to him. "Blessed are they who hear the word of God," was Mary's great beatitude, for it was above all by her faith that she was Jesus' mother. As St. Augustine says, "She was a mother by her faith before becoming one in her womb."

The preaching of Jesus was a very great mystery. Our Lord's public life was that of a preacher. His special listeners, those whose very function it was to listen to him, were the disciples: they were up front, his chosen ones. They were Our Lord's new family, and he must have aimed his words especially at them.

But when we read the Gospel we see *how* the disciples listened to and received his word: they argued—right to the very end. At the last Supper, at the very moment of the discourse that is Our Lord's Magna Carta, they were quarreling again about having the first place (Lk. 21:24). Many of their other reflections and discussions make it plain that often they did not profit fully from the preaching of Jesus. All his preaching was meant to prepare them for the mystery of the Cross; yet, when the Passion occurred, they were dismayed.

During the Agony in the Garden, the mystery lived by all of Jesus' friends down through the ages, those who were able to live it with him by being actually present, were asleep: evidently they had not understood. They who would have to preach the Cross had no sense of the mystery of the Cross: this proves that they had not listened to Our Lord's preaching in a truly contemplative way. Not until Pentecost, after experiencing the Cenacle and learning about contemplative life from the silence of the Blessed Virgin, did they receive the Spirit of Jesus, which made them Apostles. Then they first began to preach evangelically.

There is a great mystery in all this—especially in view of the fact that Our Lord, the Word of God, is the interior teacher. Exterior teachers, such as professors of theology, only present the object, the truth, whereas the interior teacher gives understanding. But when the Word, the interior teacher, came to earth, he did not follow the order that would seem logical. Before teaching the Apostles, and in order to be understood by them, it would seem that he ought first to have given them the Spirit. As master of the Spirit, he could have done so. But the mysterious fact is that Our Lord's disciples did not have the Spirit and so could not profit fully from his preaching. They did not know how to receive it as contemplatives and beloved disciples.

Light is shed on this mystery (making it all the darker, as always with mysteries) when we consider that Mary had already received the Spirit; indeed she was the bride of the Holy Spirit. When she was present for Our Lord's preaching, she took in everything, and profited fully from it. "Mary kept all these things in her heart" (Lk. 2:19).

Holy preaching is addressed to the faith of the listener, but it is a work of charity on the part of the apostle. The Blessed Virgin had to listen with faith—a loving faith animated by the gifts of the Holy Spirit, as a bride letting herself be formed by the divine spouse. Mary was the only creature who profited fully from Our Lord's preaching. (This is why the Gospel for the old votive Mass of Our Lady of the Rosary recounts the parable of the fertile soil.) Mary was immaculate and full of graces of love and intimacy; but the instruction of her faith was left to the Word made Flesh. For her faith began with no other light than that of the Old Testament.

In the holy preaching of the Church, the Holy Spirit puts on the lips of the preacher the words the congregation needs to hear. Our Lord wanted to live this mystery before we do. Hence, it is reasonable to suppose that it was in response to Mary's faith, love, and desire that many of Jesus' sayings have been given to us.[4] We should read the Gospel in this light: when he preached, Jesus was thinking particularly of Mary. Had she not been there, some of his most divine words might never have been spoken.

Since holy preaching played such a great role in the life of the Blessed Virgin, it is only natural that it do the same in the life of every contemplative. Originally it was the function of bishops.[5] One of the principal and special responsibilities of the bishop in the ancient Church was to take care of consecrated virgins and of all who lived by the evangelical counsels. (The consecration of virgins, like ordination, was reserved to the bishop.) But how better could the bishop care for these virgins than by giving them the Word of God, the only divine gift, besides the sacraments, that he could bestow?

What, then, is holy preaching? If we only knew, and if we could see how many souls hunger for God without finding the bread they need, we would implore God to raise up true apostles in the Church. It is only natural that one of the principal occupations of Dominican nuns is to pray for their brother preachers.

Holy preaching is the mystery of the Gospel lived by the Church. Just as the sacraments (especially the Eucharist), perpetuate the Passion and Cross of Jesus in our midst, so through holy preaching Jesus remains among us proclaiming the Gospel.

Instead of leaving us books, Our Lord wanted to remain

with us himself. He does this by means of a living magisterium. Divine truth, the Word, is always present with us.
This is the mystery of Our Lord's preaching perpetuated in
the Church. As in the Eucharist he continues to live his
Passion among us under the poor signs of bread and wine, so
in holy preaching he visits us and lives among us under the
poor sign of the human word. (The human word is utterly
destitute when dealing with divine mysteries).

St. Thomas says that preaching ought to arise out of contemplation and remain in contemplation. The preacher should
be engaged in contemplation even while he preaches. Words
have meaning only if there is thought behind them; otherwise
they are not signs of anything. But preaching is a word addressed to faith. It does not try to show by arguments that the
mysteries of faith are credible; rather it presents them *as
mysteries* and abides as deeply as possible in their mystery. If
the preacher is not as close as possible to his contemplation,
his word will be an ill-adapted instrument.

Holy preaching is the overflow of contemplation. But how
can our contemplation overflow when it is so hard to maintain
even a little of it in our lives? Moreover, here on earth our
contemplation is discontinuous and dark; it takes us indeed
into the heart of the mystery, but in a great darkness. How,
then, is it going to shed light? This is where theology comes
in, furnishing the preacher with a conceptual apparatus that
allows him to articulate his faith.

This, however, raises a problem. Contemplation demands
poverty of spirit, because the fire of love consumes everything. Yet theology is necessary to articulate contemplation.
(Hence, the more contemplative preachers are, the better
theologians they need to be.) We are on the way to a solution
when we realize that theology alone cannot radiate the light of
contemplation. As an acquired science, it is on a level inferior
to contemplation. Where preaching is concerned, theology is
nothing but an instrument and, as such, is very poor.

There are, therefore, two aspects of preaching, which the theologian particularly needs to keep well in mind. Holy preaching has to be the overflow of contemplation, which theology can only articulate; and there is the difficulty inherent in being an instrument. It takes courage to speak the word of God! It is hard to be an instrument and dispense riches we do not possess, which are beyond us. Such a task requires the same kind of strength as is needed to remain in the presence of the invisible.

One of the preacher's greatest resources consists in abiding in the Immaculate Heart of Mary and in her very contemplation. After Mary had lived the mystery of preaching in its fullness with Our Lord, she was given[6] St. John, the model priest.

This sheds light on many things about the Dominican Order: St. Dominic did not write any books. The task of elaborating a theology was left to St. Thomas. But Dominic gave us the Blessed Virgin. He himself did not experience the fullness of contemplation; no saint except the Blessed Virgin ever did. But St. Dominic gave and entrusted us to her, and it is the superabundance of her contemplation that will give the Dominican the audacity to preach. If his word arises out of contemplation, it is only normal that it should lead people into contemplation, producing not only believers but contemplatives. This is an instance of true spiritual fatherhood.

Thus the ideal audience for holy preaching consists of contemplatives. In them, the word sprung from contemplation terminates in contemplation and is completely enveloped by it. When a contemplative preaches to contemplatives, they live together the great mystery of preaching as a divine mission, deriving from the mission of the Word Incarnate.

In order to give an adequate explanation of preaching, we must in fact go back to the mystery of Christ's own mission in the world. The Word of God arises out of silence and returns to silence. Likewise the fecundity of preaching, insofar as it is a divine word, consists in its arising out of silence and leading to silence. Indeed, the supreme criterion for preachers is whether their preaching recollects souls or distracts them.

On earth silence, because it is interior, has a primacy over the word, which is necessarily impoverished by being expressed exteriorly. It is difficult for human words to be truly alive, since life is interior and immanent. Moreover, words are inevitably multiple and diverse.

The marvel of the Divine Word is that it is interior and immanent. By the same token it is a silent Word, implying no division. It is a unique and completely luminous Word; there is nothing to impoverish it. It is a word full of love that leaves the silence unbroken. The mystery of the Trinity is the mystery of the silent Word.

How does this apply to the mystery of holy preaching? If the good Lord permits the priest's word to arise out of the silence of contemplation and lead back to it; and if this word nourishes love and plunges us into contemplative prayer; this can only be because it is a divine word. The human word does not impart silence. Hence, the mystery of preaching consists in God's using the word of the preacher as a sign and instrument with which to give souls a taste for contemplation, and in God's permitting that word to articulate the contemplation without disrupting the silence and without the shortcomings of the human word (division, distraction, and turning back upon oneself).

Contemplatives have thus a double responsibility: to strengthen preachers by their contemplation, and to form them by their thirst for the Word. The cloister is consequently the place par excellence where the mystery of holy preaching ought to be lived. Both the preacher and his listeners are sincerely searching and both have the Holy Spirit as their interior teacher. It is in the cloister that the preacher in a sense is first prepared for combat; only later does he approach the world where he will face the struggle of giving what is not

welcome. Preaching in the cloister is a kind of private preaching like that of Our Lord, who spent thirty years at Nazareth
teaching Mary and only afterward approached the crowds.

It would be wrong to think that one should not preach in
the cloister until after having preached to the people. It is just
the other way around. It is better to begin by being formed
among one's brothers and sisters in an atmosphere of peace
and then, after having attempted to articulate one's contemplation, to be sent into battle. This is in fact what we find
in the Church—for example, in the case of St. Augustine. Be
aware, therefore, of your responsibility toward your brothers,
and pray for them.

12

The Sacrament of Reconciliation and Spiritual Direction

The two principal aids for our contemplative life are the Eucharist and holy preaching. The Eucharist is *the* sacrament of contemplatives because it is the sacrament of unity; preaching is the ever-living word of our Lord. The Blessed Virgin, we have seen, was nourished to the full on both of them.

The Church, however, gives us yet another help in the Sacrament of Reconciliation. This is above all the sacrament of sinners. It is indispensable for our contemplative life since we must live this life while being still sinners. Only the Blessed Virgin, being immaculate, was able to live the contemplative life in all its fullness; we need the Sacrament of Reconciliation.

And how can we as contemplatives profit most from our confessions? Penance is the sacrament of encounter with our Lord's mercy. In this sacrament Jesus himself, the divine physician, comes to heal our souls under the garb of his priest. He wants to give us his pardon in a very human way, through the intermediary of his minister, who will also be able to arouse our contrition and help us discern the chief obstacle to our contemplative life. The latter function is not an essential part of the sacrament, but falls within its scope, thus making the Sacrament of Reconciliation a prolongation of holy preaching.

81

Because it is a sacrament, Penance is on the level of the theological virtues. Hence, it is good to prepare for it by acts of faith, hope, and love, as well as by acts of humility. We can always show God that we have at least the desire to be humble; the very act of going to confession is an act of humility. It is an acknowledgment that we are sinners and that as sinners we live our contemplative life. Just as the Eucharist is the sacrament of unity, so Penance is the sacrament of humility.

Charity and humility are the two great poles of our contemplative life and they are proportionate to one another. Humility is the only moral virtue that enters into contemplative prayer; and the more our contemplative life grows, the more our humility must grow also. Charity is nourished by humility, for God gives himself to us to the extent that we are humble. These two virtues always develop together even though only one or the other of them may be in evidence. God, the divine educator, arranges everything in order both to humble us and foster our love. To prevent our confessions from becoming routine, we should look upon them as opportunities to humble ourselves before God.

But how should we undertake our examinations of conscience so as to profit most from our confessions? Examination of conscience is necessary for every interior life as well as for every moral life, in order to give oneself a direction and not be tossed about by whatever pressures are strongest. But the examination of conscience can be made more or less contemplatively, depending on our spirituality and our stage of growth.

If we are contemplatives (at least by desire), the best way to examine our conscience is to draw close to our Lord and the Blessed Virgin, and ask them to do it for us by the light of the Holy Spirit and not merely the light of our reason. If we desire a life that is more than just moral, if we desire to live a contemplative life—that is, a life directed by the action of the Holy Spirit—it is only natural that our examination of conscience should be made on that same level. One made on the level of reason alone would necessarily overlook a whole area of our life.

But what does it mean to ask our Lord to make the examination of conscience for us? It is something like what happens in contemplative prayer. Every friendship is a colloquy between friends; only God has no need of words since he manifests himself to us in silence. Likewise, our examination of conscience should consider everything in the light of the love of our Lord and of the Blessed Virgin; they should be our light and our judge. We should ask them to show us anything in us that has slipped out of the grasp of love and has not been directly under their dominion. In this spirit, we can review the key virtues of our contemplative life—fidelity, trust, humility—asking Jesus and Mary to show us how we may have failed in them. Such an examination of conscience is something like a contemplative prayer.

As a sacrament, Penance always gives grace. However Jesus is there as a physician—a spiritual physician—and in order to be helped by a physician we have to explain our condition to him. The profit we derive from this sacrament will therefore depend on the depth of our understanding of spiritual realities.

Thus, there are two ways to examine our conscience. One is to look at our sins from the outside, so to speak, on the basis of a list drawn up through our past experience. Then we try to arrange them in a kind of hierarchy. This type of examination is used both in confessions of necessity (for our mortal sins) and in confessions of devotion (which confess the faults that hinder the progress of our spiritual life).

But we can also examine ourselves from within, on the basis of our intimacy with God. What in our life obstructs this intimacy? Here love is our guide. In our friendship with God, have we always been present, trusting, self-effacing? In other words, this type of confession tries to cover everything in our lives that has slipped away from love, everything that has been lost to our contemplative life. It is recovered by being brought before the divine mercy. Jesus knows how to draw a greater good out of the acts of humility that we make under his guidance.

This is the truly contemplative way to examine one's conscience. It uncovers faults quite different from those disclosed by the first method. Our dear Lord does not blame us for the same things that others do.

The difference is somewhat like that between the priest in the confessional and the superior in the chapter of faults. If we examine ourselves from the point of view of intimacy with God and love of him, we will confess many small sins, even involuntary ones, because we sense that these are hindering God's work in us. If we examine ourselves in the light of our Lord's love, we will never be empty-handed; there are all sorts of natural first impulses for which we will reproach ourselves. For the contemplative life, the life of contact with God, presupposes that we let ourselves be led entirely by God; that the Holy Spirit, the Spirit of Jesus, takes the place of our own spirit. We spontaneously let him act within us, so that our initial impulses come from him. When that is the case, any first impulses that originate in ourselves are the occasion of self-reproach.

There are also faults that do not seem very serious in themselves, but have incalculable consequences: little infidelities to the Holy Spirit, little spiritual sins. The Holy Spirit comes to us delicately, like a very discreet friend. We slip into a fault so slight that we hardly perceive it; but that does not lessen its consequences. However, our Lord is always merciful; and if we humble ourselves, the Holy Spirit comes to take us back, especially if we make ourselves pupils of the Blessed Virgin and try to abide in her heart.

Moreover, the consequences of a fault are not always proportionate to its gravity. There are very evident exterior sins, such as anger and impatience, which do not have serious consequences and punish themselves by the reactions they provoke in others. There are also interior sins against ourselves that entail their own punishments; think of the remorse we feel for having been unreasonable. And there are interior sins against God or against the Holy Spirit, which imply an indocility to love. These remain completely hidden; our consciences do not reproach us for them. But these are sins in which the human ego and reason go against love, and we must ask pardon most of all for them.

These first impulses always originate in self-love but take different forms according to our temperaments. The latter reduce to two main types: (1) *sensual natures,* which are adverse to effort and look for ease and comfort, and (2) more *generous natures,* which instinctively seek to dominate to assert themselves and build up their own ego.

Let us ask our Lord to help us to detect those first impulses that prevent us from having an intimate relationship with him. Let us ask him to purify us of them. (We often tend to look upon confession too humanly, as if it were a chapter of faults or some sort of punishment. In actual fact it belongs to the realm of love.)

There are also sins of discouragement: in the contemplative life these are the most treacherous. We are speaking of discouragement in the broad sense of the term: the lowering of one's ideal, the surrender of so-called "illusions," a touch of bitterness. Under the pretext of being "realistic," or out of a false humility, one closes oneself to grace. The soul loses its original freshness and innocence, that simple trust in our Lord's predilection, which was at the origin of its vocation, and knows for sure that Jesus can return at any moment and renew his intimate presence.

What the monastic fathers call *acedia* is almost always due to discouragement; the things of God lose their savor and the soul becomes blasé in regard to spiritual matters. It is very

important to note that in such a case it may well be that
externally we have not been guilty of any faults, and have kept
all the rules—like servants. Yet we are closed and block the
life of grace within us because we forget or take practically no
account of those capital faults that sterilize our contemplative
life.

Let us, therefore, make our examination of conscience in
the light of our ideal. If we examine ourselves according to the
law, there are certain things for which we will feel no guilt; but
if it is Jesus, our love, who judges us, he will reproach us for
the slightest insensitivity.

This is the only way to make a peaceful examination of
conscience. Scruples arise when we take the point of view of
sin rather than that of love, which is that of the freedom of the
children of God.

SPIRITUAL DIRECTION

In the confessional the priest represents our Lord. He has
power over the Mystical Body and enters into the inner
secrets of the heart. Strictly speaking, confession is limited to
sin; but, given the very structure of this sacrament, it naturally tends to go beyond this limit. Great prudence is called
for here; any priest can give absolution but not every priest is
gifted for spiritual direction.

Spiritual direction is a prolongation of both preaching and
confession. Preaching gives us the words of God, direction
gives the word of God *for us*. It is preaching adapted to the
individual person. We need the priest[1] to repeat and confirm
our Lord's words to us personally, even if we think we have
already encountered it elsewhere.

Spiritual direction is likewise a prolongation of the Sacrament of Reconciliation. Strictly speaking, only sins need to be

confessed, but God often wants interior souls to tell the priest also about the graces they have received in order to have these graces confirmed.

Spiritual direction is sometimes regarded as an aid to prudence. The director is seen as an educator who forms our prudence, somewhat like a novice master. This is the style of direction normal for those engaged in an active life. In the contemplative life, however, the role of the director is much more profound and intimate. For spiritual life consists not merely in avoiding sin but above all in being docile to the grace of God and in living as contemplative a life as possible. God gives signs to help us, and spiritual direction comes in to confirm those signs from God.

Direction in this sense is situated above time, on the level of eternal life. A priest might have the role of director for only a brief period of our life, or on just a single occasion. Although it occurs in time, its value is outside time.

Here lies the mystery of spiritual direction, and here we must connect the role of director with the gifts of the Holy Spirit in us. Intimacy with God depends on an affective knowledge of God coming from the gift of wisdom. But the Holy Spirit's dominion over us presupposes that we have the attitude of a child or of a bride letting herself be loved by God; hence, a certain passivity. Someone with a voluntaristic or willful attitude is able to love, but does not let himself be loved. He closes himself in order to drive ahead. A certain weakness or littleness is wanting to him.

The gifts of the Holy Sprit, on the contrary, by their basic structure, require that we be more and more children confronting a mystery we do not understand; that we learn more and more the littleness of the Gospel, the littleness of love. But then what safeguard have we against illusion? What protection is there for someone who surrenders himself to the Holy Spirit in such littleness? Here the Church intervenes in the person of its priest. We can put ourselves under obedience to a priest, who has been entrusted with power over the inner forum of conscience. Through his ministry our interior life will thus be submitted to the Church.

Spiritual direction, in this essential function, grows all the more necessary as contemplative life deepens. The littleness required by this life needs to be backed up and confirmed by the priest whose task it is to strengthen and guard the soul, also to help it be open and poor.[2]

Because this area is so delicate, it requires priests who understand the contemplative life; otherwise great damage could be done. What we are dealing with here is a mystery. The priest's role is itself very mysterious. As Jesus in the Eucharist may be said to surrender himself into the hands of the priest,[3] so here God wills that the priest enter into an utterly private and personal domain, the inmost secret of a soul.

The graces we have received, our interior life at its deepest and truest, are much more difficult to talk about than our sins. In the first place, this matter is very private by nature. Secondly, no words are adequate for what we have to say, so that we are compelled to stammer, something that is always very humiliating. A third and deeper reason is the danger of being possessive about the graces of God.

It would be dangerous to speak about our interior life to anyone who has not the mission to deal with it, or even to speak about it to ourselves. That would be one more way of trying to appropriate God's graces. But when in the secrecy of the confessional we confide these matters to the priest, as God's representative, a great grace of silence and of what we might call "divestment" is given to us.

The priest has another task of reminding us of the graces God has given us in the past, and this presupposes an ongoing spiritual direction. The divine signs at the origin of our vocation are often much more meaningful to him than to us. God sometimes wants us to reveal secrets of his grace to the priest in order that the latter might on occasion remind us of them and confront us again with our ideal. The priest is the "friend of the Bridegroom" who reminds us of the Bridegroom's love for us. He has the beautiful role of guardian.

The priest will also help give a certain continuity to our contemplative life by supporting us in our weakness. All this is a mystery that gives us an inkling of the communion of saints. Everyone experiences this mystery differently, but all must be open to it.

Spiritual direction is one of the main tasks of a preacher. It has the same exigencies as holy preaching and presupposes, therefore, an intense contemplative life. It is why the sisters ought to pray very hard for their brothers in the ministry.

13

Study

Certain helps given us by the Church, such as the sacraments and holy preaching, are absolutely indispensable for our contemplative life. We have considered the prime importance of the Eucharist and the complementary role of the Sacrament of Reconciliation. As a sacrament, a divine sign, Penance is a sure means of purification—even in the sense of what are called "passive purifications." It helps detach us from everything that hinders our freedom of heart, the freedom of God's beloved children.

We have seen how the liturgy extends the role of the Eucharist and invests it and the other sacraments with splendor. It also makes our life more attractive. But liturgy, insofar as it is distinguished from the sacraments, is not an essential means for the contemplative life, and not all souls have the same need for it. It is necessary to recognize this.

Study can be envisaged as an extension of the liturgy; as such, it likewise is not indispensable. For it to be profitable and useful for the contemplative life, it must be approached with an attitude of respect and humility. Let us consider its role in the Dominican life.

STUDY IN THE DOMINICAN LIFE

Study can be viewed fruitfully as an extension of the teaching office of the Church. For theology submits us to the magisterium; it puts us, as it were, in the school of the Church. St. Teresa used to urge her Carmelites to pray for great theologians in the Church. The need for them is felt instinctively in contemplative souls; more than any others, the daughters of St. Dominic ought to have this intention in their hearts.

Study is absolutely indispensable for apostles; and the more contemplative they are, the greater their need to be theologians. Where holy preaching is concerned, a life of intimate union with God does not compensate for the study of theology but, on the contrary, makes it all the more necessary. This relates to what has been said about affective knowledge of God: the act of charity plays the role of the concept; hence this knowledge develops in darkness and does not give us new ideas.

Furthermore, union with God requires the attitude of a little child and a sort of death of the intellect as it plunges into darkness. This is the bride's death of love, allowing the heart to be set on fire and permitting our Lord to give himself to us. But the preacher has been called by God to articulate the fruit of his contemplation. He will therefore have to have recourse to another kind of knowledge for the concepts that will permit him to communicate those treasures that have been "loaned" to him.

Of course, the twelve Apostles did not need to learn theology, for they had the charism of inspiration. But in the normal order of things, the preacher has to place himself in the school of the Church if he is to articulate his contemplation accurately and in accord with the judgment of the Church.

The preacher takes the place of our Lord; he is the "friend of the Bridegroom." Like John he is a witness: ". . . that which we have seen with our eyes . . . and our hands have touched, this we proclaim to you" (1 John 1:1). He needs, therefore, experiential knowledge. But, inasmuch as he has to explain and articulate, he also has to put himself in continuity with

the teaching of the Church. He should be both an instrument
of the Holy Spirit and an envoy of the Church.

One of the grandeurs of theology is that it permits the
apostle to "objectify" and "universalize" his contemplation. It
allows him to present the "secrets" of God discreetly and in
such a way that they become a nourishment for all souls,
whatever be the way God is leading them.

Ideally, there should be but one theology, whereas there
are a variety of spiritualities. The deeper we go into theology,
the more objective and universal it becomes. (This is why St.
Thomas is called the Doctor Communis.) In the domain of
spirituality, however, the more we advance, the more the
needs of each soul prove to be different and the more we must
respect that diversity.

One of the functions of holy preaching is to present the mysteries of the faith. But in order for preaching to have the
doctrinal value of nourishing souls with the dogmas of the
faith, the theologian himself needs to have fathomed and
firmly grasped the great truths of faith. And the deeper his
grasp of them, the simpler his preaching will become, participating in their transcendence.

Systematic theology is, therefore, absolutely necessary for the
preacher, especially for those who preach about the Blessed
Virgin (who likewise need a greater degree of humility).

THE ROLE OF STUDY IN THE LIFE OF
CONTEMPLATIVE NUNS

Although study has not the same function in the life of the
nuns that it has for their brothers, the preachers, it is nonetheless useful both for their contemplative life and for the
apostolate appropriate to their vocation—a maternal and dis-
positive one, as we have seen. But they must never forget that

charity and humility always take first place in their lives, because these are the foundation of Christian perfection. They are necessary, therefore, here as everywhere.

Something that frequently hinders the spiritual progress of religious sisters is pride in their state. This is a somewhat pharisaical or Old Testament attitude, rather than the very humble attitude of a servant. Such religious lack a certain fire of charity and, by the same token, a certain fruitfulness.

It is very important for sisters for accept the life given them by God with great simplicity, in obedience and humility. If they find inward "satisfaction" with their office (whatever it might be); if they exercise it with the attitude of a master or superior, something of the religious life has eluded them.[1] No longer are they acting purely out of love, and they are not so well off as one who is in the lowest place.

To return to the question of study: in a purely contemplative life, it is not absolutely necessary for all, nor is it necessary at all times. The affective knowledge of God, about which we have already said so much, is a higher kind of knowledge than theology. The study of theology itself obliges us—and this is one of its advantages—to reaffirm the primacy of affective knowledge and to defend a simply contemplative life, such as that of St. Bernadette for example. Our studies, therefore, must always be done with a certain openness and, like everything else that is not the absolute, be kept within certain limits.[2]

"Openness" here means that we do them in the full consciousness that the Holy Spirit can dispense with them and give himself to us more intimately and deeply in our contemplative prayer. We ought to be ever ready to interrupt them for a while and simply remain close to him should he ask us to do so. "Being kept within certain limits" follows from the very fact that they are subordinate to something else. We should never pursue them in a purely academic manner. Our model in this is Dominic—our brother—and a saint.

THE UTIILTY OF STUDY

In mystical knowledge God develops our faith by intensify-
ing our charity. This kind of deepening involves the "narrow
way" of the Gospel. In the very act of knowing, we become
poorer, not richer, in order that all the capacities of our heart
might be taken hold of. On earth our power of attention is
limited; the Holy Spirit therefore mobilizes everything within
us in the service of love and, by plunging us into the dark core
of faith, keeps our attention from being dispersed even by the
light we receive.

Theological knowledge, on the other hand, is an articulation of the faith. Per se, theology is not supernatural; of itself it
does not deepen the faith directly, since faith is a gift of God.
Theology develops faith merely in the sense of giving it a
greater extension.

The usefulness of theology[3] lies in its teaching us to purify
the way our faith takes hold of its object. By means of analogies, it strips us of a sensory and imaginative way of thinking.
For example, St. Thomas's treatise on the Trinity provides
neither images nor illustrations. With a style completely different from that of St. Augustine, he shows the transcendence
of the faith. God is not a father in the same way that men are
fathers; eternal generation is different from human generation. This is the chief function of analogy—to show what the
supernatural is *not*. In studying theology, therefore, we try to
raise ourselves above the level of the senses; we purify our
sensibility and our imagination by means of a procedure that
is, to be sure, somewhat technical.

The study of theology is also an excellent protection against
the world and the parlor. Study withdraws us from the world;
after the dissipation inevitably entailed in outside contacts, it
puts us on another plane. It serves as a barrier or buffer
between the world and the interior life; it purifies the spirit of

the agitation churned up by the contact with the world and thus helps to dispose it once again for contemplation.

All this may sound rather negative, as indeed it is; for the function of human means in the contemplative life is precisely a negative one. But we can go further. The study of theology brings about a certain sanctification of our intellect provided, of course, that we do not strain at it nor forget that true sanctity lies in the heart, in a total surrender of the will to God. Theology accustoms us to refer the whole intellectual world back to God, to see everything in the light of God's transcendence. It forms in us a way of thinking that centers our intelligence on God, so that we see everything in God's light and on the level of eternity. But a deep-seated disposition of the intelligence—what St. Thomas calls a *habitus*— takes over our whole mind, which is why it is not possible to excel in two *habitus* at the same time. Hence, by orienting our whole intelligence toward God, theology can help us greatly to recover the presence of God when we have lost it.

Furthermore, theology impels us to make our faith explicit and to take stock of its riches. This presentation of the objects of faith supports our contemplative life; for it is very difficult to maintain a right intention without being supported by a knowledge of the truth. To be sure, the support given by theology is nothing in comparison with that which the Holy Spirit can give us interiorly through love. But when the Spirit is silent, this presentation of the doctrines of faith can sometimes be a help. Hence, even though this explication of our faith is not indispensable to the contemplative life, it is a help and we should not disdain it.

In order to profit from the study of theology, we must do it with the right attitude. This can be difficult because theology, as a work of the mind, is a type of wealth. And because it is so close to God, we can easily become too attached to it; for the closer human goods are to God, the greater our danger of

becoming attached to them (for example, friendships that are
very supernatural).

Theology is a type of wealth because it forms us into "masters." In fact, it is the function of every intellectual discipline
to make us "masters" by putting us in possession of a *habitus*.
This is part of the value of theology, but also the source of its
danger for contemplatives, because it does not teach us how to
become like little children or like brides of the Holy Spirit.
There may be masters in theology, but not in prayer! However, theology can make us love the simplicity of prayer just
by contrast.

Another danger, or a different aspect of the same one, is
pride. It will help to understand it if we consider the temptation of the angels; for theology is the most angelic of human
activities.

The temptation of Lucifer was to remain in his own natural
excellence, disregarding the secrets that God wanted to reveal
to him. God asked him, the master, who had the role of
illumining lesser spirits, to accept the truths of faith and thus
become a disciple. Such a posture emphasizes trust and
fidelity in regard to God and requires the acceptance of truth,
not for its value as knowledge or for the perfection it brings to
the intellect, but because it unites us more deeply with God's
own knowledge.

God was asking Lucifer to become a servant in a way that he
was not by nature, but Lucifer did not welcome this opportunity. His sin did not consist exactly in disobedience; he knew
only too well that God was his master, to whom he could not
refuse anything. Rather his sin consisted in a kind of inatten-
tion; he was so taken up with his own riches, he did not pay
attention to God.

It is somewhat the same with us. When the Holy Spirit
comes as a very discrete friend, asking us to trust him, and in
poverty to accept the secrets of his heart, if we are too caught

up in our theological riches, we are likely to overlook him, or to place little value on what he offers.

We also experience a certain fear of the poverty and death intrinsic to love itself. From the standpoint of reason, theology is in a sense a surer way. Our anxiety about how the life of study and the life of prayer can be reconciled is at bottom fear that God will take too much from us. This is the real difficulty. These two ways of knowing are fundamentally diverse; we cannot have at one and at the same time the attitude of the theologian or master, and the attitude of the spouse or little child. The only solution is to trust God. We cannot know in advance what the right combination of study and contemplation will be in our life, but the Lord will work it out; let us leave it to him.

In conclusion, let us put our studies in a truly contemplative atmosphere, an atmosphere of profound prayer. The more we gain from our studies, the more intense our prayer has to be. Hence, the prayer we say before beginning our study is very important. Like St. Thomas, we should love to stop from time to time to ask for light: even the most speculative of our studies can only benefit from a sense of the things of God. Let us never be afraid to mingle prayer abundantly with our studies and to give God plenty of room.

Humility is also necessary—humility before God and humility also respecting others less intellectually gifted than we are, but who perhaps receive more intimate graces of prayer. We must not close ourselves to them or adopt an attitude of rivalry or jealousy, as if other peoples' union with God were a hindrance of embarrassment to us. On the contrary, let us regard ourselves as their servants.

Finally, and above all, the Blessed Virgin can help us much in this area because she herself is a milieu of humility and intimacy. Our Lord was the greatest of theologians, but Mary's knowledge of God consisted chiefly in that of intimate union.

Let us ask her, therefore, to preserve a childlike attitude in us. This is one of the reasons why the Dominican Order was entrusted to her.

If we have problems of conscience about our studies, let us ask her to solve them. Above all, let us ask her to give us confidence in those lights that God may give us during our studies. Very often we fail to have sufficient recourse to her in this area.

14

The Vows and the Contemplative Life

The contemplative life is the normal unfolding of the life of grace within us. It is a very special type of life, one that dates from the time of our Lord.[1] It is in the strictest sense a life according to the Gospel. Since it requires that our charity become as perfect as possible, it is greatly helped by the religious state, as a school of perfection.

The full development of charity, both in its essence within us, and in its outreach to those around us, requires the practice of the evangelical counsels. But every true Christian is bound to practice the counsels to some degree, and all Christians ought to be imbued with their spirit at least. We could therefore be tempted simply to make private vows to live the evangelical life interiorly, without entering the religious state.

Let us try to see, therefore, what is so special about the religious state and the public profession of vows in the presence of the whole Church. There is a certain tendency these days to minimize the value of religious life in favor of private vows; hence it will be useful to try to discern the peculiar value of religious profession and public vows, as well as the special obligations they entail.

By our profession we commit ourselves to live in community a way of life that is centered on the practice of the evangelical counsels. The Church vouches for this way of life by approving our constitutions. Generically, then, religious life is simply a regime of life inspired by counsels; what makes it different from a life under private vows is the fact that the Church rather than ourselves presides over its structure.

When speaking of the mystery of the Church we have recourse to the analogies of the family and society. The religious life is a cell of that family or society that is the Church. It is modeled on the Church, as the Church is modeled on our Lord. The Church puts its stamp of approval on religious orders so that they might be representative of the life of the evangelical counsels, and thereby reveal a particular aspect of the mystery of the Church.

Like the Church, therefore, the religious community is a family and a society. But it is very different from earthly families and societies, and problems often arise from our failure to make the necessary transpositions. Earthly families are based essentially on procreation and therefore on consanguinity. That is their strength and also their weakness. In the religious family, we are born "not of the flesh nor of the will of man but of God" (John 1:13); likewise, we do not choose one another; it is God who chooses us. Neither family ties, nationality, social status, nor affinity bind us together, but only the grace of God, who has chosen each soul individually. Each of us has received the same call, but we did not discover it together. It is God's will that has assembled us.

Since the contemplative life does not require any natural predispositions, there can be a great diversity among us. The good Lord can bring together people of very different temperaments; in fact he seems to delight in doing so. For we have a witness to give: we profess to live a life of charity. In order that our witness may be all the more convincing, God sometimes trusts his religious to such a point that his love alone unites them; they are in agreement on nothing but the contemplative life. This is not rare among those who are specially entrusted to the Blessed Virgin; as an educator, she is extraordinarily bold.

Even while being deeply united in regard to the ideal we serve, we can cause one another much suffering in other respects. This should not surprise us, but should stimulate our confidence and hope, impelling us to long for an even greater mutual charity. "Let us love another in charity"—that is, in full truth and very deeply. Let us show our Lord that we love one another because we love him. Our vow of chastity is very important here, for our communion with one another is based in large part on the bond it forms among us.

THE BOND OF THE VOW OF CHASTITY

The unity of earthly families is rooted, as we have said, in consanguinity. In religious families, however, unity is based on spiritual generation—that is, the call or choice of God. And the vow of chastity safeguards this unity in the same measure that it safeguards the perfection of charity—charity as regards both respect for each one's vocation and genuine unity or compenetration of hearts.

The vow of chastity keeps our hearts free in order that they might be given first of all to God and, while belonging to God, might also, in an apostolic order, be given to others. The vow of chastity, therefore, is not restricted to purity; for purity, to be a virtue, must be ordered to charity. Chastity must not be viewed in a merely negative way. To commit oneself to a celibate life in order to avoid having a family, or to preserve one's independence, or to acquire a certain freedom of mind propitious to our work, a certain peace and solitude of soul in which we are our own masters—this would not be the same thing as the vow of chastity.

The latter implies that one truly loves God more than all else. One's heart must be given wholly to God and, in God, wholly to others. The vow of chastity also supposes a very great detachment of heart; it allows God to determine the order among our friends. Instead of having personal preferences, we adopt our Lord's choice and we are free to love those he asks us to love.

The vow of chastity also implies a great respect for one another, which is lacking at times in earthly families (where vocations are not always respected). As virgins consecrated to contemplation you have, as one of your first duties in charity, to help one another live the contemplative life and to avoid anything that would hinder another's intimate union with God. It is from this point of view that one ought to look at the question of silence in action and in speech. Many customs that at first seem obsolete flow with strict, inner necessity from the need for recollection.

Think of the common life of Mary and Joseph. Their home was both the first cloister and the first family of the Church; it was a house of contemplation. Let us ask the Blessed Virgin to give us the spirit whereby we too might be a family entirely ordered to contemplation and to the spiritual maternity flowing from it. Let us ask her to make our monastery a house of contemplation (the radiance of which will make our house apostolic).

The vow of virginity also helps guarantee that nothing but God will be the basis of our unity, it preserves us from "particular friendships" (i.e., possessive and exclusive bonds) on the one hand and from jealousy and pettiness on the other. God gives us the grace to live a common life that is at the same time very free and intimate, because animated by the charity of hearts that are free.

Because the religious life also entails poverty and obedience, and because it is made up of persons, each having his or her particular vocation, the religious community is also a little society. It cannot be understood adequately when viewed exclusively as a family.

However, a religious community is very different from earthly societies. The stability of the latter comes from private property, which permits each family to have its own life and each person to take root and develop as a person. According to St. Thomas, private property is necessary because it encourages initiative. The stability of a religious society, however, is based on the two closely connected vows of poverty and obedience.

We do not take the vow of poverty merely in order to have a life of poverty. We do, of course, need detachment from the goods of earth; but the deeper intent of this vow is to suppress the attitude of private ownership that "incarnates" a person in the world by the extension of himself in his possessions. We take the vow of poverty in order to keep from getting "settled in." (Thus we do not rent our cell or work for hire.)[2]

But why do we take the vow of obedience? What is its connection with poverty? Private property exists in order to encourge the greatest possible development of initiative and, therefore, the formation of powerful personalities. The vow of obedience aims at making us submissive and having us maintain all our life long the attitude of a little child or a servant. In this it is closely connected with poverty, it defines a state of servitude.

To understand the nature of religious obedience, we must distinguish it from two other forms. There is first of all the obedience of the child (to which that of a disciple can be likened). Dictated by prudence, this allows a child, by participating in the wisdom of its parents, to lead a truly human life and develop into an adult. Secondly, there is the obe-

dience of the citizen, dictated by legal justice: we all benefit
from the common good and are in turn bound to observe the
law promulgated in view of the common good. Thirdly, there
is religious obedience. It cannot be justified on the grounds of
prudence except perhaps during the novitiate, but much less
or not at all thereafter. There is no obligation to believe that
our superiors have a more perfect vision of the ideal than we
do, or that they are necessarily the best guides for our interior
life. (Dominican priors do not have the same function as
abbots of a monastery.)

Neither can religious obedience be accounted for in terms
of legal justice,[3] but solely in terms of love and of the desire to
follow our Lord and to imitate his life (". . . go sell all that you
have and . . . come, follow me"—Mt. 19:21). Our Lord was
obedient unto death, death on the Cross; and it is our love for
Jesus that justifies our vow of obedience.

We have tried to give God everything. But the inner gift of
ourselves can be made only in the present moment, instant by
instant. Hence the Church puts at our disposal a means by
which we can give ourselves to God more completely; and not
only our earthly and bodily goods, but also those of the spirit.
Human greatness derives from the fact that we are masters of
ourselves—of our time and our actions, and that we are capable of governing ourselves and the world. Obedience allows
us to make a holocaust of our lives, to be servants out of love
by following the will of Jesus as it is manifested by our
superiors. It is a servitude, but a sacred one very close to the
Cross of Our Lord.

By the vow of obedience we give everything pertaining to
our exterior life, along with that which is deepest within us—
namely, our own will. Together with the vows of chastity and
poverty, it puts us in a state very close to that chosen by our
Lord himself. It is very favorable to contemplation and ele-
vates our exterior life to the level of our contemplative life.

Viewed from this angle, the religious life is one that will
never fail us; we can always have confidence in it.

HOW TO PRACTICE OBEDIENCE

The practice of obedience varies from one order to another.
What makes obedience difficult for cloistered Dominican
nuns is the fact that their whole life is regulated by a rule,
their time cut up into small bits, and they are bound by
customs not chosen by themselves individually. This kind of
obedience bears on very little things and can be quite mortify-
ing.

For the friars, obedience does not function the same way.
The apostolate requires that they be allowed a certain liberty.
But the preacher never knows what is going to be done with
him, whether he will remain in the monastery of his choice,
whether he will have the kind of life he would like. Will he be
sent to Rome or Jerusalem? Will one who desires to preach be
asked to teach?

In this case the demands of obedience are more difficult,
and perhaps more profound, due to the fact that we ourselves
are not the only ones involved. The spiritual bonds we have
formed can sometimes make a change of monasteries more
difficult than leaving one's family. They entail suffering not
only for ourselves but also for others—souls who seem to need
us. At times it is as if we were sacrificing them for God. Such
acts of detachment are very difficult for the apostle, and
sometimes demand very great acts of faith.

In your monastery, these two ways of practicing obedience
are combined. There is the obedience demanded by a life
governed in detail by a rule and also, because you belong to a
congregation, that of a life that can be totally changed by your

being sent elsewhere. In such trials one must make an act of faith and think of our Lord, who saved souls more by his death than by his preaching.

Let us ask the Blessed Virgin to help us; she, above all others, is our model in the religious life. (Our Lord was not a "religious" nor even a "wayfarer"; he did not have to strive for perfection, for he was already perfect.) Because of her fullness of grace, Mary was by rights a queen from birth. Yet her condition was always that of a servant. She was submitted first to St. Joseph, then to her son and, finally to St. John. She was always in someone else's house, in a state of dependence. It is she who will teach us how to obey.

15

The Great Enemy of the
Contemplative Life

Since nature does not have to furnish any predispositions for the contemplative life, the greatest obstacles to this life do not come from our nature. The obstacles that arise from within us are not on the same plane as our contemplative life. Our proper enemy is Satan; being a pure spirit, he *is* on the same plane as contemplation.

It is a simple fact of experience that it is especially in monasteries that the devil tries to sow trouble. While he has lost the love given to him at creation, he has not lost his intelligence; and he is well aware of the strategic points of the Church. He leaves to his henchmen the task of unleashing the various forms of concupiscence in the world and trapping souls by them; he takes direct personal responsibility for the more difficult objectives—namely, contemplatives. He is their personal enemy, especially of those who have entrusted themselves to the Blessed Virgin.

At first glance it seems rather strange that Satan should have been completely unaware of the Blessed Virgin while she was on earth. Having lost grace himself, he did not recognize her greatness. We see in the Gospel that he attacked our Lord and the Apostles Peter and Judas, but not Mary. Since there was in Mary perfect harmony between nature and grace and between flesh and spirit, it may be that her contemplative life was able to remain completely interior and hidden. In us, because of our weaknesses, the contemplative life always lets itself be perceived to some degree. Also in Mary's case there was perhaps some special permission of God; in any case, it seems that our Lord did not want the devil to take note of Mary.

If that is so, we can understand his rage on the day of the Assumption when Mary was revealed to him as the Queen of Justice; both the outrage of his natural intelligence of having been deceived perhaps for the first time, and his rage in seeing her take the place that once had been his. He discovered then the greatness of her motherhood. Now he seeks to attack Mary in her children both out of hatred for her and because he understands that they are very dear to Our Lord.[1]

It is important to see clearly the devil's objectives in this battle in which the Blessed Virgin is our commander-in-chief. Our faith and our personal relationships with God do not imply a real combat so long as we are submissive to God. The devil, therefore, does not attack us head-on; he seeks, rather, to trouble souls by every possible means, even those unworthy of a pure spirit.

The contemplative life demands a great deal of confidence. Since the intimate knowledge of God grows only in peace, contemplatives are particularly vulnerable to disturbance. The contemplative life is very delicate, a life in faith and in darkness; hence it lacks the security that comes from seeing for oneself. This makes our lives very vulnerable to disturbance the moment we become separated ever so little from the hearts of Jesus and Mary.

Within this sanctuary, in the deepest part of our souls, the devil cannot act. This is the domain of contemplative prayer in which the Holy Spirit alone is master. The heart of Jesus is an impregnable fortress for us. The devil's strategy is to try to make us leave this fortress of love and lead us onto the field of imagination or of false lights, where he can attack us.

As there is a special presence of God in monasteries, there is also a special presence of the devil; that is why the Church blesses those places. When we feel ourselves vaguely troubled without there being any evident reason, we should ask the Blessed Virgin to free us from the devil; often that will be enough to restore our peace. Rather than trying by ourselves to ward off imaginations and reasonings that trouble us, we should take refuge in Mary. Otherwise we may simply stir up our feelings, which is exactly what the devil wants. He cannot act directly on our wills, but he can make use of our feelings, either by instilling anxiety into them, or by pushing them to extremes and to a violence they do not naturally have. Whereas the Holy Spirit acts in the depths of our soul by love, the devil acts on our feelings by creating disturbance.

The devil was created for contemplation; the contemplative life is, therefore, normal for him. Along with his intelligence, he has retained a sense of the contemplative life; only it no longer blossoms into love. Having rejected God as his supernatural end, he can no longer find repose in God. He has, therefore, no place of rest, not even a natural one; that is why, as St. Augustine says, he wanders about the world like an intruder.

We can understand his hatred of religious, poor human beings who by nature are not made for a purely contemplative life as he was, but who by grace now possess what he rejected. Knowing only too well the demands of contemplation, he makes every effort to impede it by creating disturbance.

His second objective is to sow the tares of dissension and division. It is easy for him to do this for the only basis of total and permanent union among contemplatives is the love of God; as soon as we step outside that love, there is occasion for division. As a result of his sin, Satan has fallen into the realm of division, and he seeks to draw us in his wake.

The remedy is very simple. We should always try to come back very humbly into our Lord's presence and into his peace. We should follow the example of the saints and not seek to flout the devil or even look at the temptation. If we stay on his level, we are always in danger of being defeated: "Satan is an admirable dialectician." But we have a defense against which he has no weapon: faith, trust, love, and docility to the Holy Spirit. As long as we are in the domain of contemplative prayer with the Blessed Virgin, we are safe; as soon as we leave it, he can do with us as he will. We must never want to play with him, not even to insult him. This can be a subtle temptation, and it is very dangerous, for he is intelligent and powerful.

One of Byron's characters asks Satan, "Are you good?" "I am beautiful," is the reply.[2] The devil is certainly not good, but he *is* beautiful. He will try to tempt us with his beauty, and we can let ourselves be seduced. The children of the Blessed Virgin should avoid acting as children of Eve: abstain from curiosity, and not play games with Satan. Rather, they should follow Mary's faith, obedience, and humility.

16

Conclusion: Life in Mary

During this retreat we have tried to live the mystery of our contemplative life. We have seen that its focal point is that wholly intimate knowledge of God given to us in the darkness of faith and in a kind of death of the soul. Hence, the necessity of three fundamental attitudes: (1) *humility*, which opens us up to the gift of God; (2) *confidence* in his love of predilection for us; and (3) the *fidelity* of the spouse who accepts everything.

We have to live this life of intimacy within the Church, for it is in and through the Church that we receive our faith. It is, therefore, very important to use the means the Church puts at our disposal: (1) *sacred preaching*, by which we are instructed as beloved disciples and which is prolonged in the more human science of theology; (2) the *sacraments*, sources of life, the chief of which is the Eucharist, *the* sacrament of the contemplative life; (3) the *liturgy*, which provides a sacred framework within which to live the *evangelical* counsels. The latter give us a family based on the vow of virginity and a society based on the vows of poverty and obedience. Thanks to these vows our lives do not become merely a series of actions undertaken for the sake of God but a sacrifice; and this puts our activity itself on the same level as our contemplative life.

Now let us ask, how can we live our contemplative life *in*

the Blessed Virgin? How can we place ourselves under her tutelage and remain there? And is it right to do so?

From what has been said about it during this retreat, the contemplative life would seem to be extremely simple—but also very difficult, precisely because of its simplicity. Mary alone, because she was immaculate, was able to live the contemplative life perfectly; it is only natural that we be called to live it in her.

But does the phrase "in Mary" designate something real, or is it merely a metaphor? If real, how can it be achieved?

THEOLOGICAL FOUNDATIONS

We must recall the essential aspects of the mystery of the Blessed Virgin. God chose her to be the mother of his Son, but also to be mother of us all, the new Eve. She had a uniquely intimate relationship with Our Lord as associate and beloved mother.

Mary's motherhood is mysterious. She was specially chosen by God to be his mother. Like all of God's choices, the choice of Mary implies a mysterious predilection.[1] The great sign of God's predilection for her was the Immaculate Conception, a fullness of grace derived not from any merits of hers but solely from God's good pleasure.

How much did God love his mother? More than the Apostles? More than all the saints? More than the new Jerusalem? That is God's secret. However, since grace is the fruit of God's love, we have an indication of his love for her in the Immaculate Conception, Mary's fullness of grace.

Theologians who have studied the mystery of Mary's fullness of grace generally agree that her final grace (at the moment of the Assumption) surpassed not only that of the angels (Mary took Lucifer's place) but also that of all the angels and saints combined.

God did not want to sanctify Mary as a creature—that is to say, within certain limits—or as a part (even though the principal part) of the Church. He willed to sanctify her as a whole, as "a world in herself," as St. Bernard says. He gave her a fullness of grace that was indeed finite in comparison with that of our Lord, but which had a kind of infinity in comparison with the grace given to us. He wanted her to be like a universe in herself, with all the graces that have been given to any of the saints recapitulated eminently in her.

Many theologians hold that even Mary's very first grace surpassed in its plenitude the consummated grace of all the angels and saints combined; but on this point, agreement is not so general. In any case, one's initial grace is like an interior law that gives one's spiritual life its peculiar rhythm. This leads to the important consequence that, because of the immensity of her initial grace, Mary's spiritual life developed at a rhythm different from that of the angels and saints. This too is a great mystery.

Some great Marian doctors hold that Jesus wanted to create for himself two masterpieces: a people and, among that people, a mother who would be the bride of his soul and absolute queen. (The latter point implies that all the elect exist for her sake just as she exists for the sake of our Lord.)

Let us briefly consider how the plan of the Incarnation unfolded. Even before the coming of Jesus, Mary already had his Spirit, although she still belonged to the Old Testament. Hers was the role of final preparation for him: an intense longing for his coming. Out of respect for human freedom, God did not want his Son to come to earth without being wanted. Mary's longing was sufficient, springing as it did from a heart that was already maternal, since her fullness of grace had been given entirely in view of her motherhood.

At the Annunciation, Mary had to be there in order to say *fiat*—"let it be done"—in the name of the whole human race, as its queen. Throughout our Lord's life Mary was there, both as a witness who, knowing what was going on, profited fully from him and as a beloved mother who, on earth, took the place of the Father in heaven.

After his Ascension she was left to watch over the beginnings of the Church. Immediately after her death, without waiting for the Last Judgment, she was glorified as queen in body and soul. From then on, heaven has been constituted by the human natures of Jesus and Mary; and Mary thus reunited with her Son has been his instrument in the government and salvation of the world. In one and the same love they saved us and in that same love they now sanctify us (cf. St Louis de Montfort).

Our spiritual life must therefore develop in the light of this truth. Since Mary has a fullness of grace, it is truly the will of God that we, who will never have anything but partial graces, remain in her. We must abide in Christ de jure, for his fullness of grace was absolutely infinite. We must abide likewise in Mary de facto, for her fullness of grace was infinite, not in itself, but by comparison with ours. Our life of prayer will never surpass Mary's, for we have no grace of intimacy with our Lord, however deep or varied, that she has not already known.

It follows that our attitude towards the Blessed Virgin ought to be quite different from our attitude toward the saints. The latter can introduce us to the interior life, but they can never be our masters; the Holy Spirit alone is our master. Each soul has to a certain extent its own spirituality and its own special friendship with God. Hence the other saints do not intervene in the true moments of truly intimate prayer. When we attain genuine friendship with our Lord, the friend who led us to it stands aside. This is true even of our father, St. Dominic: we do not lead our life of prayer in his.

But Mary is truly the mother of our contemplation; the deeper we bury ourselves in her, the more intimate our union with Jesus. Of course this intimacy will not always be explicit; faith implies a veil. But if the good Lord leads us into the heart of the Blessed Virgin, asking us to put our trust in her and to live for ourselves that intimate relationship she had with our Lord; if he gives us the certitude that in her we are very close to Jesus, we can be completely at peace. This is what we will all experience in heaven, and God wants to give us a foretaste here below.

We should always be very free in our contemplative prayer. To say that we must always go from Mary to Jesus and from Jesus to the Blessed Trinity is to look at things too materialistically.[2] God may bring souls into the heart of the Blessed Virgin after first having led them to the Blessed Trinity, and then to our Lord, to his Cross, or to his Sacred Heart. Whether we are with the Blessed Trinity or the Lord or the Blessed Virgin depends entirely on the will of the Holy Spirit.

Of ourselves we cannot attain the Blessed Trinity except by concepts or created ideas; only in heaven will we be able to see it directly. But if, without suppressing the mystery, our Lord wills to share with us the contact and intimacy that he, as a man, had with the Blessed Trinity; and if, while hiding from us the vision of the Father, he takes us into his heart and makes us relive the way in which he loved the Father with his human heart, we are then much more closely united to the Trinity than we could ever be through the images we fashion.

If Jesus asks us to imitate the humility he displayed during the months that followed the Annunciation, by hiding our contemplative prayer in the heart and bosom of Mary; if he invites us to trust in the love and intimacy she had with him, and to remain in that intimacy; we can be sure that intimate union with the Father and with Jesus himself[3] is being given to us in her holy heart.

If we are in contact with the Blessed Trinity (without per-

haps being explicitly aware of it) simply by remaining in
Mary's heart, by reliving her intimacy with the Trinity, this
involves extra humility. We are obliged to trust in Mary's love
for the divine persons, to trust that in her heart we will find
everything. But we are infinitely more united to the Trinity
this way than through the lights proportionate to our own
degree of grace.

If fidelity to the Holy Spirit and to love leads us to the heart
of the Blessed Virgin or to that of our Lord, we must let
ourselves be led. Our prayer then becomes simpler. There is
more love in it; we are more captivated by the grace of Jesus
and by his heart—that is, by the very center of his love for us.
He wants us thereby to remain close to him, in the kind of
death proper to the bride. He may also wish to share with us
his own intimacy with the Blessed Virgin. We must let him do
as he pleases.

The subject matter of prayer is of little importance; what
matters above all is the degree of our love. We must realize
that if, in terms of love, God gives us everything, he often
gives us little in terms of light. The domain of knowledge here
below is always limited; only in heaven, in the beatific vision,
will knowledge be complete.

God can ask us to be very humble and to make an act of
faith in the way by which he leads us. We must abandon
ourselves to him and not be dismayed if he leads us first to the
Blessed Trinity, then to our Lord and his Sacred Heart, and
finally into his intimacy with the Blessed Virgin. God's good
pleasure must be respected above all else. This is the right
way to envisage life in Mary.

It is significant, moreover, that, while the Church has not
defined Mary's mediation, it has directed our attention toward
the mystery of her Assumption. This directly concerns our
Lord's attitude toward Mary, for it proclaims her union with
him in glory.

It is thus that the Blessed Virgin is presented to us in the rosary. For the rosary is made up of all the mysteries of our Lord's life; we try to grasp them in the same way that Mary herself grasped and lived them.[4] This is a more contemplative way to live them, a very intimate way in which we recapture the state of soul and the very sentiments of the Blessed Virgin. This is how to live these mysteries with her, and she will always lead us into that very intimate knowledge of Jesus and the Father.

We must always let the Holy Spirit do as he pleases with us. Nevertheless, seeing how important Mary is, we have the right to ask our Lord—if we have understood these things—to give us a deeper understanding of this mystery, to lead us into that intimacy with Mary which he himself had, and to let us experience a little of the trust he had in her.

If we already have his attitude and have already been introduced into the heart of the Blessed Virgin, if, in short, we are her children, we have every right to remain in her heart and make it our place of prayer. We can adopt an attitude of docility toward her for the rest of our lives. Because of the union of Jesus and Mary in heaven, docility to her is one and the same thing as docility to the Holy Spirit.

With such an outlook—humbler and less prone to illusion—it is easier to know the will of God. If Mary wishes to make us live her docility to the Holy Spirit, we will be infinitely more docile to him in and through her than by ourselves. She will give us a very strong spirit of obedience along with humility. (Even a child who has not yet the use of reason, can, if obedient, behave like an adult.)

If we are very obedient to the Blessed Virgin with this virile obedience and with love, even though we have not yet acquired the virtues and are still full of faults (but are at least detached from them), it may be that she will allow us to live her own contemplative life, the contemplative life of the Immaculate One.

Notes

Foreword by Jean Vanier

1. This is Mr. Vanier's suggested translation for what is rendered in the text as *holy preaching*. See note 1 to chapter 11.

Editor's Preface

1. Two of Dehau's works, *Rivers of Living Water* (London: Black-friars, 1957) and *Eve and Mary* (St. Louis: Herder, 1958) have won him a small but appreciative circle of English-speaking readers. More of his works have appeared in French, and others are still being prepared for posthumous publication.

Chapter 2 / The Purpose of the Dominican Order

1. The last sentence of this paragraph came second in the original text.
2. This does not mean that they *are* perfect, but only that their state obliges them to tend toward perfection (*Summa Theologiae*, II-II, 184, 4, 5).
3. St. Thomas holds that Christ commissioned the Apostles, and through them bishops, both to preach and to baptize. But preaching they were to do themselves, as their principal office, whereas baptism they could entrust to others (*Summa Theologiae*, III, 67, 2, ad 1).

Elsewhere, St. Thomas distinguishes four kinds of religious instruction: that which aims at converting to the faith, that which imparts the elements of the faith, that which teaches people how to live the Christian life, and that which is concerned with "the deep mysteries of the faith and the perfection of the Christian life." The first can be done by anyone, the second belongs chiefly to priests, the third to godparents, and the last pertains properly to bishops (ibid., III, 71, 4, ad 3).

4. The author is assuming the traditional view that each of the sacraments was instituted specifically by Christ. Modern historians tend to qualify this view.

5. In characterizing the contemplative apostle as an instrumental cause and other apostles as secondary causes, the author is employing some classic distinctions of scholastic philosophy that may not be familiar to most modern readers.

First, there is the distinction between principal and instrumental causes—for example, between the carpenter and his tools. When the carpenter makes a chair, he is said to be the principal cause of it, while his tools are instrumental causes. They too produce the chair, but only in a subordinate way; they act, but only in virtue of the carpenter's action on and through them.

A second distinction, not to be confused with the preceding, is between primary and secondary causes—that is, between God, the First Cause of all things, and creatures, which are only secondary causes. For it is a classic principle of Thomistic metaphysics that creatures can act only insofar as they are moved by God, the "First Mover" in all movement. However, this does not mean that creatures are nothing more than instruments (which would reduce this second distinction to the first). Creatures have real powers of action and real initiative. The carpenter is the principal cause of the chair, not just an instrumental cause. Even though his action is constantly dependent on the influx of the divine "First Movement," he is not thereby reduced to the status of a mere instrument. The distinction between principal cause and instrument, between the carpenter and his tools, remains intact, even though both carpenter and tools are only secondary causes, dependent on God, who is primary.

Such are the notions the author is using in an attempt to express the distinctive character of contemplative preaching. He contends that whereas in ordinary (or "active") preaching, the preacher acts as a principal cause (albeit under God's prime causality), the contemplative preacher acts as a mere instrument. In other words, active preaching has the same metaphysical structure as any other natural human activity. Man, using his mind, his feelings, his talents and all his other natural human resources, plus the light of faith and, let us hope, the inspiration of the Holy Spirit, does a work that is properly his own. He is not a mere instrument of God, even though he is serving God. Bishop Sheen's sermons, if they may be taken as an example, were truly and properly Bishop Sheen's work, even though ultimately God is to be praised for whatever was good in them.

But contemplative preaching is much more radically dependent on God. The preacher is not the proper cause of the effects produced; he is only used by God for a work that is directly and properly the work of God. He is not only a secondary cause (like all creatures), he is a mere instrument. Not that he is inert, lacking in freedom, and no more responsible than a puppet. Rather, he may be compared to the inspired authors of Sacred Scripture. According to the paradoxical but classic Thomistic interpretation, they are free instruments. They use their own natural resources, even while being employed by God as spokesmen. Their word is truly theirs, even though at a more profound level it is the Word of God. Similarly, the contemplative preacher is truly preaching his own sermon; but God is making use of it and making it productive.

No doubt, God can make use of any human activity, even evil deeds, to produce effects quite unintended by the human agent. In such cases it is also true that the human being is used as an instrument. But unlike such examples, the contemplative preacher is a *willing* instrument of God. He voluntarily surrenders himself to be used by God, and makes it his whole endeavor to be available for whatever God wishes to do through him.

This makes a radical difference in the spirit or psychology with which he works. The active apostle has the psychology of a principal cause. He considers persons to be evangelized, their attitudes and habitual motivations, and accordingly employs whatever resources he has to bring them to the desired goal. The contemplative, on the other hand, has the psychology of a simple instrument: his principal effort is to let himself be used by God.

This does not mean that the contemplative apostle closes his eyes to his human audience and looks only to God for inspiration. It is extremely difficult to express adequately the delicate distinction being presented here. Perhaps it can be said that the contemplative is, on the human level, just as active and just as much of a principal cause as the active apostle; but that the contemplative at the same time remains constantly attentive and surrendered to God, so that his natural activity is subsumed and employed by a higher activity coming from God. Although he speaks and acts on his own, still he can accomplish nothing toward the apostolate except insofar as God uses him. And if it be retorted that the same is true ultimately of every apostolate, it remains that there are two different *psychologies* of the apostle.

6. The original text simply mentions Catholic Action as an example. As the specific nature of this type of apostolate may not be as present to the reader's mind as it was to the original audience of this retreat, I have added the explanatory phrase, "apostolate of like by like."

7. The original text here added three pages on the special contemplative vocation of Les Tourelles, the monastery in which this retreat was preached. Being of less interest to a more general audience, they have been omitted.

Chapter 3 / The Mystery of the Contemplative Life

1. In the original text, the sentence, "The principal . . . virtues" came at the beginning rather than at the end of this paragraph.

2. In the original text, this paragraph came one paragraph earlier, after the question, "As long as we are on earth, can we be contemplatives in any other way than by desire?"

3. In the original text, this paragraph came after the one that now follows it.

4. The text here reads "spiritual." I take this to be a slip on the part either of the preacher or the one who took the notes. It would make the sentence irrelevant to the theme being treated, as well as contradictory to St. Thomas, who holds that spiritual sins are far more serious than carnal sins, with which he contrasts them in the

Summa Theologiae, I-II, 73, 5. I conjecture therefore that the author intended to say "involuntary sin," but I have not located his reference to St. Thomas (which is I presume freely paraphrased, according to the author's usual style).

Chapter 4 / The Contemplative Life: The Special Call of God and the Fundamental Attitudes of the Contemplative

1. Faith is here understood as belief in what God has revealed. In its normal form, it has as it *object,* a truth that has been formulated—e.g., in the Apostle's Creed. Infused contemplation, on the other hand, although based on faith, is directly mediated by a union with God in love, as is explained in the present chapter. Thus qua knowledge, it is not so objective as simple faith.

This is said without prejudice to the possibility of "implicit" faith, in which the object of faith is quite hidden or confused, instead of being articulated clearly in a creed.

2. "Information or"—added by translator.

3. On the meaning of the religious state, see chapter 14.

4. The last six paragraphs have been rearranged from the original text.

Chapter 6 / Prayer

1. The clause, "Whereas an order is the act of one who is in full command," as well as the phrase, "given by human reason," in the preceding sentence, have been inserted by the editor to clarify the allusion made here.

2. In the original text, these first two sentences came at the end of the paragraph.

3. Instead of "praise God," the original text here reads "give thanks"; but the logic of the argument seems to call for the change I have made.

Chapter 7 / The Contemplative Life: A Mystery of Faith

1. In the original text, this clause reads literally "this is a dogma." At first sight, it would seem to refer most naturally to the fact that

the object of faith is presented to us by the magisterium; but it could also refer (especially if we suppose that a link or two in the chain of thought escaped the notetaker), to the articles of faith as presented by the magisterium. I have adopted the latter sense, because it makes a logical connection between what precedes and what follows.

2. The first half of this paragraph has been simplified somewhat from the rather complicated original.

Chapter 8 / Hope and Difficulties of the Contemplative Life

1. The clause, "We would like to create unity in our lives," came after the first sentence of the preceding paragraph in the original text.

2. Literally: "somewhat materially."

3. The clause, "as can be seen from . . . sorrowing," came three paragraphs below (in the paragraph, "Such antinomies . . .") in the original text.

4. "Total renunciation of our intellect" does not mean that we cease using it altogether, but that it abdicate its pretension to be the sovereign ruler of our lives. The will of God is the supreme law for us, and before it any contradictory counsel of our own prudence must give way. But that we use our reason is part of God's will for us; moreover, it is only by our minds that we come to know God's will.

Chapter 9 / The Sacraments and the Contemplative Life

1. Even though our liturgy is eucharistic, so that it is important not to separate the sacraments from the liturgy, it is important to distinguish between them, at least in my personal opinion. (Editor's note: The foregoing note formed part of the original text, where it occured four paragraphs below, right before the paragraph, "Authentic Christian spirituality. . . .")

2. The sentence, "Liturgy is what . . . on the Eucharist," has been composed by the editor from elements scattered through the paragraph in the original text.

3. The sentence, "It would seem . . ." has been inserted by the editor on the basis of other writings of Father Philippe.

4. In the original text, the sentence, "If Mary . . . immaculate," comes at the beginning of the next paragraph.

5. Literally, "provision for a journey," a term used traditionally for the Eucharist given to someone on the point of death.

Chapter 10 / The Liturgy

1. In the original text, these last two sentences followed the opening sentence of the following paragraph.

2. Allusion to Tobit 12:7, "A king's secret it is prudent to keep, but the works of God are to be declared and made known." This is the classic scriptural text cited by spiritual writers in discussing the question, which graces ought to be disclosed for the glory of God, and which ought to be kept secret out of humility and discretion.

Chapter 11 / Holy Preaching

1. This name is a literal translation of the expression *sainte prédication*, used by Father Philippe. It is admittedly unsatisfactory, because too generic (as is also the French original). It does not imply that other kinds of preaching are unholy, but simply that this mysterious function, in which the preacher relives the mystery of the preaching of Jesus and, under the inspiration of the Holy Spirit, nourishes the faith of his hearers, is holy par excellence.

Holy preaching does not adequately indicate the specific nature of such preaching, but neither does any other term I can think of. I was tempted to called it *sacred preaching*. This sounds less generic than holy preaching, but has liturgical connotations not desirable here. *Spirit-filled preaching* gives part of the idea; however, other kinds of preaching may also be inspired by the Holy Spirit. In the foreword to the present work, Jean Vanier suggests *preaching from the heart*. This too reflects one aspect very well, but neglects others. In the absence of any decisively better name, I have kept to a plain, literal translation of the original. To understand better what is meant, one must read this chapter (and, even more important, one must have had some experience of the reality itself).

2. In the original text, the second and third sentences of this paragraph were in inverse order.

3. The original text here adds, "Holy preaching is an essential function of bishops, because they are in a state of perfection." This alludes to the teaching of St. Thomas Aquinas (*Summa Theologiae*, II-II, 184, 5) that the episcopacy is a state of life that entails a solemn obligation to do what is demanded by Christian perfection. He illustrates this by the fact that a bishop, as pastor, is obliged to lay down his life rather than desert his flock.

As this doctrine of St. Thomas, and the very notion of state of perfection, have become unfamiliar to most modern readers, it seemed better to omit this sentence, which could not be explained and justified without a rather lengthy treatise.

4. In the original text, the third and fourth sentences of this paragraph were in inverse order. Note also that the Gospels allude several times to a group of women who accompanied Jesus and the apostles. In Acts 1:14, Mary is mentioned apparently as one of them.

5. See note 3.

6. The original text says here, "was given to. . . ."

Chapter 12 / The Sacrament of Reconciliation and Spiritual Direction

1. It is not indispensable that the spiritual director be a priest. Most often this seems to be the case, however, and there are definite advantages to this arrangement, as indicted in the text.

2. The last half of this sentence, "whose task it is . . . ," originally came at the end of the next paragraph.

3. The clause, "may be said to surrender himself into the hands of the priest," has been inserted by the editor to clarify the allusion.

Chapter 13 / Study

1. This teaching could easily be misunderstood. It is not meant to imply that religious should be perpetually dissatisfied with their work! Nor that the joy that arises from any good work, and most particularly from the service of God's children, detracts necessarily from the purity of love animating the work. *Satisfaction* is meant here in a very strict sense, as the sense of fullness and contentment

we derive from that which gives our life value. As indicated in the text, it leads a sister to do her work with the attitude of a master or superior rather than that of humble servant.

2. ". . . be kept within certain limits" is an attempt, admittedly unsatisfactory, to render the original, *revêtir un mode particulier.*

3. The author has in mind here scholastic theology, and specifically Thomistic thelogy. What he says would not apply to historical theology, nor to most of other theological styles current today.

Chapter 14 / The Vows and the Contemplative Life

1. Although one can speak of contemplatives in pre-Christian cultures (after all, it was Aristotle who gave us the term *contemplative life*), Christian contemplation is specifically different from all others, as this whole book shows.

2. The original text here reads literally "pay for our work," which I assume to be a mistake.

3. I believe that this statement is to be understood in terms of a fully adequate account. For religious living in community, the demands of the common good, and therefore legal justice, do give grounds for a certain obedience to superiors. Not, however, for the kind and degree of obedience cultivated in the religious life. Only the reasons given in the text suffice to justify this.

Chapter 15 / The Great Enemy of the Contemplative Life

1. Cf. Apoc. 12:17.

2. I have not been able to find this text in the works of Byron. The only passage I could find that in any way resembles it occurs in the dramatic poem *Cain*. When Lucifer comes onto the stage, Cain asks him, "Are ye happy?" and Lucifer replies, "We are mighty." Father Philippe does not read English, so it could have been only in translation that he encountered Byron. As he was not much given to the reading of poetry (this is the only poetic allusion I can remember him ever making), it is probably a citation made by someone else in a philosophical or theological work that he is recalling. Moreover,

Father Philippe's citations are always very free, even when drawn from his favorite author, St. Thomas Aquinas. But whether or not this is an accurate quotation is utterly unimportant to the idea being advanced.

Chapter 16 / Conclusion: Life in Mary

1. The first two sentences of this paragraph stood originally at the end of the paragraph.

2. The second and third sentences of this paragraph were originally in inverse order.

3. The original text here says literally "that all of this intimacy is being given to us in that bosom, in that heart of the most Holy Virgin."

4. The original text here inserts the phrase, "We are all the more in faith," but I am not sure in what sense it is intended.